D0734326

career
stages
OF CLASSROOM
TEACHERS

Betty E. Steffy, Ed.D.

career stages
OF CLASSROOM
TEACHERS

TECHNOMIC
PUBLISHING CO., INC.
LANCASTER · BASEL

Career Stages of Classroom Teachers

a **TECHNOMIC**®publication

Published in the Western Hemisphere by
Technomic Publishing Company, Inc.
851 New Holland Avenue
Box 3535
Lancaster, Pennsylvania 17604 U.S.A.

Distributed in the Rest of the World by
Technomic Publishing AG

This book was written in Dr. Steffy's private capacity and the
expressions of opinion are not necessarily those of the official
policies of the Kentucky Department of Education.

Printed in the United States of America
10 9 8 7 6 5 4 3 2 1

Main entry under title:
  Career Stages of Classroom Teachers

A Technomic Publishing Company book
Bibliography: p.
Includes index p. 211

Library of Congress Card No. 89-50504
ISBN No. 87762-637-5

VALHN

Table of Contents

Introduction

Since the first Monday of June, 1859, six hundred and forty-two temporary, and twenty-five professional certificates have been granted. It cannot be reasonably expected that among such a large number, of every age, from fifteen to fifty, all are *good*. Some are poor, some middling, and some very good. A majority are making laudable efforts to improve in their profession.

Extrapolated from the annual report of the County Superintendent in *Report of the Superintendent of Common Schools of Pennsylvania for the Year Ending June 4, 1860.*

Written of teachers by Charles R. Coburn, Superintendent, Bradford County, p. 27.

THE teaching cadre is composed of all sorts of teachers, and anyone around or near them would echo Superintendent Coburn's observation made over a hundred years ago.

Yet, contained in Superintendent Coburn's report lies the common fallacy of dealing with the teaching cadre, which is, that the differences among and between teachers regarding their performance as teachers can be ascribed to some sort of objective state, and that certain treatments can be applied to remedy unsatisfactory performances.

So the history of the teaching profession in America is laced with county institutes, professional meetings, required courses, normal schools, methods courses, and ultimately staff development.

This book began as a simple observation, learned from trial and error, that something more profound was at work within the teaching cadre. We've known for a long time that teaching as a career attracts people with certain outlooks. Most teachers are expected to love children though not all do, at least in the same way.

For a long time, teaching was a first-choice career for women and a second-choice career for most men. Men went into teaching because they couldn't be doctors or lawyers. Women went into teaching because there were not very many things a woman was allowed to do in a sexist society. Teaching was respectable. Historically, men were more militant and conservative as teachers, whereas women were more liberal, flexible, and compliant.

But something else at work is the *effects of teaching* on the teachers. I've chosen to call this the "infrastructure," which refers to both the way the work is shaped and accomplished, and the rules and the division of labor in schools. At the heart of the infrastructure lies the control of what teachers do and the boundaries of their decision-making authority.

As teachers work within their roles and within schools, their orientation toward work, their ideas of self, their vibrancy, and their enthusiasm undergo changes. Indeed, there appear to be some definite orientations towards work which I have called "stages," that can identify teachers at a particular time in their careers. I've chosen to break them up as I've encountered them as a teacher, director of curriculum, assistant superintendent, and finally, as a superintendent. At this point, I'm not totally sure I like all of the titles I've assigned to them, but that's not so important as the idea that there are "stages" per se. Also, there may be more or less than I've described in this book. The number of stages may also be open for more discussion, probing, and perhaps some formal studies about them.

I have found that by understanding where teachers are in their internal growth and then shaping professional activities and altering working conditions, the investment of a school system's resources are better spent, and the results are more positive.

Over the years, I have shared these ideas with teachers. I have listened to not only what they say about themselves, but also to what they don't say about themselves. Both are important. I have also experimented with changing working conditions that seem to correspond to a particular teacher's need at any given stage.

My experiences tell me that the stages are identifiable and that they are changeable. I have also found that some teachers remain fixed at some stages for long periods of time, especially if there is reinforcement for a particular stage. When teachers recognize where they are, they can take steps to change their own orientation towards their work, especially if they have supportive colleagues and knowledgeable principals, supervisors, superintendents, and board members.

Yet, within all of these individual responses lies a larger responsibility with those that govern school districts, define work rules, and shape working conditions in the schools. There is too little understanding of the long-term deadening impact that much legislation has on teachers. My own experience as superintendent has convinced me that much legislation aimed at enhancing teacher productivity actually has the opposite effect. Standardization and routine may initially produce some glitter, but in the end they are "fool's gold," because all they produce is paper and very cynical adults who have to produce the paper, as well as teach. The isolation of teachers in the cellular structure of schools makes the temptation to become dull too easy to resist. Routines breed dullness over time. And it is the effect of time on teachers that leads to sharp differences among them in schools.

Traditional staff development fails to deal with this problem, firstly, because it accepts too much of the present working conditions as inevitable, and secondly, because it doesn't differentiate among teachers based on their own internal focus at any particular time. In short, traditional staff development fails because it is stageless. Not only is "a teacher not a teacher not a teacher," as Dwight Allen used to say, but "the same teacher is not the same teacher is not the same teacher," over time. A teacher's internal orientation to teaching is not stable. Rather, it is fragile, permeable, regenerative, and expandable. Because teachers are human, their orientation to work is renewable.

This book was written because schools are at the same time no better or worse than the least able teacher. It is because teachers remain the one indispensable, yet most mysterious, resource that exists in schools that this book attempts to explore and improve teaching by not separating the teaching act from the teacher. At any given time, where the teacher is, is where the school is. The two states are identical.

This book is dedicated to the many teachers with whom I have worked: Marcia Arkin, Lynn Schilling, Gretchen Greer, George Ferris, Bob and Dory Allen, Carol Smitten, Al Nous, Terri Freed, Al

Tanner, Ina Logue; and to the administrators who supported my own professional renewal: Bern Seiderman, Julia Desmone, Evelyn Ogden, and Al Solomon.

More than anyone else, teachers have to keep believing that humanity is worthy of education. A teacher's own humanity is the cornerstone of that faith. Without that faith, tomorrow arrives without hope.

Betty E. Steffy

chapter
ONE

Re-Conceptualizing Contemporary Challenges to Classroom Teachers

IT'S WHAT'S INSIDE OF TEACHERS THAT COUNTS

ANYONE who has been a teacher, worked with teachers and shared their trials and tribulations on a day-to-day basis, understands that many of the differences among teachers with respect to their orientation to work is internal. What is inside teachers, what they carry in their heads and hearts, keeps them coming back to the classroom day after day, in spite of unappreciative pupils, meddlesome parents, or indifferent administrators.

Motivated teachers can accomplish near miracles, overcome obstacles that their less-dedicated colleagues would find debilitating or demoralizing. Teaching has been called the lonely profession, because under most circumstances, it is done with only children as the watchers. They may or may not be immediately responsive. Unlike a courtroom lawyer who "does his thing" before a judge, jury, and the press; a history teacher's brilliant summation may not be noted until years later, if at all. Rewards in teaching are thus intangible and often delayed; they are intrinsic rewards. It is the intrinsic rewards that are actually motivational (Herzberg, 1966) and that matter most (Lortie, 1975). This organic approach to a career, however, is most often missed in discussions about motivating teachers or improving teaching.

The model of this book is called "the career stages model." It is based on the premise that what keeps the fire burning bright inside a teacher is internal. Therefore, important changes in what teachers perceive about their roles and what continues to keep them going are fundamentally anchored in their internal orientation to work.

Motivating teachers is not so much a challenge of imposing some

1

new approach such as merit pay or career ladders (Burden, 1987), but is getting inside of teachers' heads and emotions to understand how they perceive their own world of work.

People enter the teaching profession for many reasons, but money is not one of them. Complaints about low pay are historic and chronic; they extend back into the nation's educational history for hundreds of years. Teachers may leave teaching not only because of low pay, but also because of working conditions. If teaching were a "cream puff" job, the pay wouldn't be such an issue. But when both pay and responsibilities are considered, the effort in the classroom may pale in comparison to easier jobs with more pay.

And of course, sexism has played an important part in keeping some female teachers in the classroom. For a long time, a woman could be a secretary, a nurse, or a teacher. Women who aspired to anything else for an honest living were not realistic and certainly not feminine. So talented women kept following the road to the classroom, despite both low pay and abysmal working conditions. The saying was, "teaching is hard, but the pay isn't bad for a woman."

While teacher working conditions have emphasized the privacy of the job, the teaching work force views the general arena as a cooperative endeavor. Judging by work task complexity, teaching has not been highly interdependent; therefore, teachers have not developed a culture that is critical of what they do collectively (see Bidwell, 1965). Because of this condition, there has been a tradition of non-critical review in education, unlike what one might find in the art world or other professions. This tradition has emphasized cooperative working mores and discouraged those which appear to be negative or destructive. Almost all teachers view evaluations of themselves as negative and punitive. At least *part* of this perception is due to the lack of a strong tradition of training in professional criticism and reflective discourse. There are no enduring case studies of great teachers in action to which novices aspire. Teaching is intuitive and repetitive from generation to generation. The influence of a great teacher is largely on his or her students; it is not shared in any lasting technical sense with colleagues who may come after the great one's retirement. The calling of teaching is not to attain technical brilliance, but to "do good" with kids. There is a fundamental difference between teaching and many other professions. It serves to discourage criticism, blunt administrative control via evaluation, and buffer teachers from having to worry about the total flow of each other's work in a school (see English, 1987).

The reality is that the teacher is absolutely alone and only minimally connected to the work of other teachers. Thus, the teaching cadre stands only for a loose group of fellow practitioners, each one working separately from the others. The implication is that while teachers may share similar complaints about their work, the work can be improved only by treating them as individuals. It further emphasizes the importance of knowing where individual teachers are as individuals and not treating them as one defined group with a common technical culture shared and understood by all. That condition simply does not exist.

The Classroom as a Place of Work

As a workplace, the classroom has special kinds of pressures and problems. The dominant problem in this work place, like most others, is control over the work. If the work deals with inanimate objects, control concentrates on the statistical prediction of input, or the entry to the workplace prior to the beginning of work. Such control is absent in teaching. The teacher has little control over the input prior to the students' allocation to a classroom. Control within the classroom largely rests upon creating workable social groups that engage the students in a structured sequence of work tasks. The teacher is expected to know how to shape these tasks so that children learn in the conventional sense in which the word is understood.

Despite the fact that it is acknowledged that children are never the same, the classroom and school organization are predicated upon the similarities, not the differences among children. There is in almost all schools and classrooms a great deal of repetition (see Bellack, Kliebard, Hyman, and Smith, 1966).

While repetition is a key to economy and control, it is also the key to job boredom. Over an extended period of time, repetitious tasks become less challenging. Less energy is expended. Excitement wanes. Enthusiasm slackens. Like any other human being on a repetitious job, teachers can get stale. They can lose interest. Like robots, they can go through the motions, and a lot of teachers do just that.

As teacher zeal wanes, student response is less positive, perhaps even negative. Some teachers who don't experience professional renewal or change, may simply "lose it." They become a sad case of a "has-been." If it happens to great athletes, dancers, opera stars—why shouldn't it happen to teachers? The difference is that few athletes, dancers or opera stars have tenure. But tenure isn't the problem! The problem is that the conditions which reinforced teacher motivation on the job aren't there anymore or don't elicit the same response as they once did.

Too many schools are staffed with stale, burnt-out teachers. They may become laced with rigidity and loaded with cynicism. There are few poisons as strong to young, energetic and creative minds. Dull students are the products of dull teachers; and dull teachers are produced by schools which require conformity, stability and a routine above all else. Schools require schedules, and schedules in turn require repetition. It is hard to schedule learning; it is much easier to schedule teaching. Learning is difficult to predict; teaching however, can be quite predictable. This is not the romantic criticism of schools that was so popular in the late sixties by such writers as Kohl (1974) or Goodman (1962). It is meant rather to try and understand what happens to teachers in their workplace and why we see some of the problems in teachers that develop over time.

Few people enter the teaching field disenchanted or cynical. Many develop that orientation with time. This orientation is a reaction to what teachers find in their workplace. They find isolation in a real, physical sense. They find schedules and bells. They find requirements for mandatory sections of a state or local curriculum which must be taught. They find school administrators and supervisors whose primary duty is to ensure that they conform to these requirements and teach the curriculum. And they find an evaluation system geared to determine how well they do all of the above. Teaching today is a far cry from Mark Hopkins at one end of the log and a student at the other. Schools have become systematized and the trends all point to more system, not less. The major goal of such systems is predictability, which is purchased at the price of spontaneity. In this sense, teaching is less fun today than perhaps twenty years ago.

The Age of Accountability

Accountability as a concept bloomed in the late sixties and we are still feeling its effects. Most simply put, it means that schools (and teachers) are responsible (though they do not always fully control the variables) for what students learn. Prior to this idea, schools were responsible only for teaching. If students didn't learn well, it was their own fault. They weren't motivated. They didn't come to school. Their parents weren't supportive or didn't care. We still hear these words today. However, with accountability, the idea is that all of these factors may be so, but the school is still responsible for what children learn.

Comparing schools of twenty years ago with those of today, one can see enormous differences. One obvious difference is the presence of testing. The respective states have embarked upon an ambitious program of testing children: first in the basic skills and then in many other areas of the curriculum. Test results are in the public domain. They are as public as the Friday football score, and it is no small wonder that the pressure and problems with such visibility have multiplied. Charges of "teaching the test" have surfaced now and then to remind teachers of the temptations involved when the public visibility of their work is increased.

The testing trend will continue. The chief state school officers have agreed to a common school test to which children in the fifty states will inevitably be compared (Fiske, 1987). When average test scores of Texas are compared to average scores for California or Florida, we can expect reactive legislatures to consider all sorts of new bills aimed at predictability and compliance.

Accountability has ushered in a demand for sharper and more detailed evaluation systems of teaching. The Madeline Hunter model of teaching, despite protests by the originator, has been slavishly encapsulated into bureaucratic checklists and applied to all teachers, new and experienced, regardless of their place in the development of classroom expertise.

The application of such attempts at uniformity has been met with various forms of teacher union resistance. The first time a veteran teacher who enjoyed a digression with his class was marked down for "birdwalking" by a new assistant principal, recently trained in the Hunter technique, the seeds of dissent were sown.

In the past, one of the attractions of teaching as a career was that a young idealist could work with children and be afforded a safe harbor in the pursuit of truth or beauty. Tenure protected the teacher in search of truth. However, tenure no longer affords any teacher the option of "doing his own thing" behind closed classroom doors. The door has been pried open with public testing and left permanently ajar with state-imposed curriculum requirements.

In some states, curriculum laws require that planned courses be developed with performance or behavioral objectives for the course, designated evaluation techniques stated for each objective, and time delineations for each activity. The appropriate texts must also be cited. Such plans must be kept on file for examination by a state official on demand.

Some states have adopted the concept of external auditing by lottery or design in which school systems are reviewed for compliance with state curricular mandates. One result is that school administrators and supervisors are edgy about permitting very much deviance by the staff from the adopted curriculum packages.

Despite the fact that teachers are isolated and physically shielded from each other, this very separation means that individually, they are terribly vulnerable to pressure from administrators. They have not developed any collective control over their own work (Lortie, 1975). Once the classroom door is pried open, the idea of the classroom as a kind of privileged sanctuary is violated.

The various forms of accountability have permanently changed the infrastructure of schools, and the nature of teaching as it has been conceptualized for the past one hundred years or more. Any plan for the revitalization of the teaching cadre which does not acknowledge this fundamental fact is, at best, naive, and, at worst, merely irrelevant and wasteful of much time and energy.

TRADITIONAL STAFF DEVELOPMENT PROGRAMS

Traditional staff development contains six generic steps (Rebore, 1982, p. 170). The process, which begins with school district goals and objectives, includes a needs assessment which presumably is a discrepancy analysis of those competencies possessed by staff and those required to deliver the stated goals and objectives. From this discrepancy analogue, the administrator develops goals and objectives for a staff development program. The program is then shaped to include the goals and objectives to be delivered and evaluated.

There are several problems with this model. The first problem is that the staff is developed to fit the objectives of the district. Even if it were possible to develop the staff this explicitly, the step avoids examining differences among teachers that would be important indicators of their willingness, receptivity, or even technical competence to undergo development.

The whole idea of being developed in this sense views teachers as inanimate objects, without a free will, or without the means to decide to refuse to use what has been explained to them in the process of being developed.

Because teachers have a free will and are isolated and alone in their work, acknowledging their existing orientation to work is critical to improving their work.

One traditional means to ensure teacher compliance to packaged staff development is to employ more supervision in the form of principal or supervisor observation time. Even if this model were appropriate in school settings (and there is evidence to indicate it is not), most school districts simply can't afford to get the span of control ratio down to anything that is truly manageable (one to nine or twelve).

If a typical secondary teacher taught 180 days for six periods per day, that would be a total of 1080 total periods for a school year. In most situations, a principal is permitted three full periods of observation (by contract) for probationary teachers. Three periods is less than 1 percent of the total time a teacher would be teaching in any given year. To arrive at a minimum of 1 percent of the total time available, a principal would have to observe almost eleven full periods. No principal has that amount of time to engage in actual observations since his/her span of control exceeds that which most business schools advocate by a large margin.

This simple but nearly universal situation prohibits anything like close supervision as it is understood in other work settings. For at least 99 percent of the time, teachers will probably continue to work alone and unsupervised. Couple this statistic with the irrefutable fact that once the door is closed, teachers can decide, unilaterally and without interruption, what to do with their students. Staff development which does not account for the teacher's undisputed control of the workplace, founders on an obvious iceberg. Too many do just that.

For many administrators directing staff development, the tendency is to make no distinctions among the teacher work force. Staff development is seen as a good thing and good for everybody. Large group lectures are still a dominant mode of teacher in-service activities. Teachers are told and told and told. Staff development using a "telling" model works with too few teachers and usually the wrong ones. The cynics still sit in the back of the room reading the sports page or grading papers. The already motivated staff "tune in." The unmotivated staff "tune out."

This model of staff development focuses on goals and objectives which are considered apart from the teachers who are supposed to acquire them. It is as though the behavior could be separated from the whole person. Unfortunately, one cannot obtain a behavior without the whole person "behaving." When a person is directing an activity and considers only the desired objective, it is too easy to relegate the humans involved to the status of rats in mazes. It is, after all, behavioral psychology that underscores staff development as it has been practiced in schools.

Traditional staff development communicates a negative attitude by suggesting that a) development is necessary only at the time that staff development personnel dictates and b) nobody is developed who does not want to be developed. The behavioristic model of staff development relegates feelings, perceptions, and self-concept, as either nonexistent or minor interferences in the process. The model of staff development in this book is predicated on the idea that nothing happens unless and until the administration is familiar with the teacher's concepts. This means dealing with the whole teacher and not just his or her behaviors.

FROM STAFF DEVELOPMENT TO HUMAN DEVELOPMENT

The behavioristic orientation of staff development soon gives way to human development. It makes little sense to try to improve the technical skills of a teacher apart from the way a teacher feels about himself/herself. A teacher who feels guilty about overeating, is chronically fighting with a spouse, or flirting with drugs or alcohol, may use technical skills destructively to reinforce his/her existing mind-set and work orientation. That would be tragic.

Human development is based on the premise that one begins with the person, the whole teacher. Behaviors are simply very limited extensions of a belief system, a concept of self and an orientation to life and work which can be misinterpreted as well as correctly gauged. Behaviors are not ends, but means to ends. The end is a confident, competent, energetic and vibrant teacher who positively impacts children as a real example of living and learning. This inspirational, inquisitive, and dynamic teacher is the kind every parent wishes his or her child to encounter. The fact that there are some good teachers in schools, means that human development is possible; the fact that there are apparently so few indicates that we have a long way to go in improving the teaching cadre.

BARRIERS TO CONFRONT AND OVERCOME

As history amply demonstrates, the solution to some problems begins with conceptualizing them differently (Kuhn, 1962). One of the solutions to improving the performance of the teaching cadre is to change the way we think about it.

Recognize That Teachers Approach Teaching with Different Motivations Which Change During Their Careers

A person wants to be a teacher for many different reasons, which determines how he will respond to his job situation.

Let us consider the case of six people who aspired to a career in teaching:

Sally M. wants to have a family. Her husband is a pre-med student. As soon as her husband finishes his internship and opens a practice, she wants to have children. She likes teaching, but right now it isn't uppermost in her mind. She doesn't want to get a master's degree, because they can't afford the expense. She is content to enter teaching for a short time.

Ralph P. wants to be a poet. He found that writing doesn't pay well, and he had to have something else to support his poetry habit. Teaching offers Ralph the summer months to stroll the beaches, watch sunsets, and think about eternity. He feels it won't be too taxing on his energy or his resources.

Mollie T. has always wanted to be a teacher. Her earliest memories were of her favorite teachers, and she is determined to be just like Mrs. Quivers, her fifth grade teacher back in Evanstown. Mollie has volunteered in all sorts of activities to acquire teaching experience. She has read a lot of books about teaching. She's already planned where she will get her master's degree and she can hardly wait to have her own class.

Ken E. wants to be a lawyer, but he has few resources and doesn't know if he can pas the LSAT to get into law school. He needs something as a backup in case he is not accepted by a law school or can't afford to go even if he is accepted by one. Teaching English seems to be something he could do until he can resolve his career and financial problems.

Wayne S. wants to coach basketball. He was a starting forward in high school and at State U. He loves the game and really gets a natural high from coaching kids. He knows that he must also teach since few schools will hire just a basketball coach. He decides to minor in social studies so he can teach government classes and stay on the basketball court.

Eileen B. was married at eighteen. At twenty-two she had four children. Now as the last of the kids enters kindergarten, she wants to finish her college education. She's tried pharmacy and found it boring. She then majored in home economics and found it unchallenging. At last she thinks that maybe teaching might be her cup of tea. She knows she has to decide on a major.

All of the people above are real teachers today. However, not only were they different when they started, but what they wanted out of teaching was also different. They all responded differently to staff development.

Let us now consider these six teachers at a later stage in their careers:

Sally M. is divorced. She had to support three kids. Teaching became her profession. She went back to college to obtain a master's degree. She is considered an outstanding teacher and is president of her local teachers union. She is a seasoned union pro and a tough negotiator.

Ralph P. nearly quit teaching his first year because it was too taxing. Finally, after several years, he decided to devote his full energies to teaching. He acquired a Ph.D. and is now teaching English at a large eastern university. He has written two books on Victorian poets.

Mollie T. burned brightly for five years and then she suddenly lost interest. She came to school unkempt, put on a lot of weight, and is often absent. She never married. When she is in school, other teachers avoid her because she is quarrelsome and cranky.

Ken E. has always been a marginal teacher, and apparently he never wanted to be a better one. He's been married twice, but doesn't seem to be happy. Most of the time he sits in the faculty room, drinking coffee and reading yesterday's papers. He bad-mouths everyone and everything.

Wayne S. became tired of coaching. He had not realized how pushy parents could be if they thought their sons were not played often enough nor played properly. He was glad to get away from the visibility and the pressure. He was chairman of the social studies department for two years, but resigned because he didn't like all of the paperwork. Now he puts in his time and waits until the summer when we works as a handyman and small contractor around town. He gets a lot of pleasure from just fixing things and helping people.

Eileen B. found herself in teaching. She got a master's degree and trained student teachers. Today she is an enthusiastic elementary principal in a very posh school district. Her school is her home. She is remarried to a colleague principal; they travel together in the summers and write articles for professional journals.

Imagine all of these teachers sitting together in the school auditorium listening to Professor Smith from the local university lecture them on a topic such as "The True Meaning of Being a Professional Teacher." What effect do you think that lecture would have on these teachers, given the little we know of them from the vignettes in this chapter?

At what point did *Mollie T.* get burned out? Before or after Professor Smith's speech? Just when did *Sally M.* become serious about being a professional teacher, before or after Professor Smith—before or after her divorce?

Was *Wayne S.* a good chairman in spite of the paperwork? When he resigned as chairman, did he also quit trying to be a good teacher? Did anybody notice? Was it before or after Professor Smith's lecture?

Many teachers know from their own experience that they all entered teaching with one frame of mind and many of them changed their minds after they spent some time working in schools. No one thing was ever good for all of them at the beginning, in the middle, or at the end of their careers.

How shortsighted is it to begin thinking about improving teachers and their performance by assuming that the trick is simply to do a "needs assessment" between the difference in their skill levels and those required to deliver district objectives?

Reject Approaches Towards Improving Performance That Fail to Deal with the Whole Teacher

This proposition is not simply the opposite of the first. On one level of belief, it is possible to accept the fact that teachers are different throughout their careers but also to overlook that belief by insisting that all teachers participate in staff development sessions or career ladder plans that result in teachers being cast into one undifferentiated blob.

Re-thinking teacher performance improvement demands an expanded view of the teacher. It means recognition of the whole human being: focusing exclusively on one part may not change that part, because the part is influenced by the whole. A teacher is a whole teacher and is changing as a whole or not changing very much at all.

Start with the Human Element and Move to the Organization's Goals

Traditional management thinking envisions an abstract organization with goals and objectives, but real organizations don't exist that way. Instead, they are made up of people. In schools those people are teachers. In real organizations, people act first and then they see what their actions have accomplished (see Weick, 1985).

The kind of abstractions that administrators normally develop and boards sanctify, rarely lead teachers in their classroom duties (Dreeben, 1973). Instead, they usually embrace a full range of teacher options. The organization is still whatever teachers make of it. Starting with teachers is not a violation of sound organizational thinking and planning. It is, in fact, putting the planning process on a more rational level than before.

Re-Conceptualize the Relationship Between the Individual and the Organization

If a teacher is an alcoholic, the school system must deal with the problem of alcoholism prior to dealing with teaching competence. As more and more school districts accept the responsibility of employee assistance programs, a teacher's heretofore private life becomes the concern of the organization.

While teachers may enjoy being considered fully human and being the basis of organizational action, they also expect that artificial barriers that separate a private life from a role responsibility will disappear. The relationship between a person and the organization becomes more closely linked. It is impossible for an organization to care for a person as a whole human being without knowing about the whole human being.

Perhaps the most visible modern example of this is the dilemma and tragedy of teachers with AIDS. A teacher with AIDS cannot be expected to seek assistance from the district to continue teaching without students, parents, and colleagues inferring he is either a hemophiliac, a drug user, or a homosexual.

Neither teachers, nor the school boards for whom they work, can deal any longer with only parts of a personality. The whole person is either motivated or not. Once accepted, there is no turning back.

Recognize That the Burden of Change Is Not All upon the Teacher, But Also Includes the School System and Its Officials

Traditional staff development assumes that the teachers should be fitted to the organization. The fact that the organization may be imperfect and may be a cause of the problems the staff development program is supposed to solve is not considered. The organization is absolved. The burden of change is therefore placed squarely and exclusively on the teacher. Suppose the organization is sick? Suppose it is filled with dysfunctional relationships, and is politically corrupt, or both. Should staff development fit healthy, independent people into a structure that is unhealthy and requires dependence in order to succeed? Traditional staff development leaves those doing the developing out of the equation. Human development includes everyone and the system itself as a possible recipient of corrective action. There are plenty of things school districts can do to improve human performance, including changing the rules of the system itself. But the system has to be considered part of the problem from the outset. The goals and objectives of the organization let most school systems off the hook and make teachers the sole culprits of poor performance. This kind of logic should be rejected as a kind of ad hominem tactic that reinforces mediocrity. The proper mind set ought to be "We are the problem and how are we going to arrive at a solution?" That attitude is markedly different from "they are the problem and we have the solution."

Concentrate upon Intrinsic Motivators Rather than Extrinsic Satisfiers

Herzberg (1966) has identified those factors that are purely job satisfiers as opposed to job motivators. According to Herzberg, salary is not a motivator, but a satisfier. Giving money to people doesn't mean they will be happy or motivated, it may only mean they will complain less about money. What motivates people is achievement, recognition and visibility. Money is expected to follow, not to lead. Merit pay plans do not motivate, nor do career ladder plans. Almost all treat teachers as an undifferentiated mass, moved only by dollar signs. The absurdity of this approach is that teachers do not enter teaching for money. What turn-around would then motivate them for money? If a teacher has become sour on the job because of the lack of intrinsic fulfillment on a day-to-day basis with children, how will money change the situation?

Money is the solution where money is the problem. This should not be construed as an argument that teachers should not be paid well. They are not well paid now. Increasing the amount teachers are paid compared to other societal occupations may attract a larger pool of talented people to consider and enter teaching, but if the job conditions remain the same as they are now, money won't make them happy once they are in teaching.

Likewise, career ladder plans that are not appealing and don't include intrinsic job motivators, are not likely to increase teacher performance, because they are not inherently motivational. They are much more likely to be institutional and bureaucratic than anything else. It is unlikely that more bureaucracy will significantly improve education.

SUMMARY

Part of the answer to significantly improving teacher performance in school systems is re-conceptualizing the problem of performance. Performance pertains not only to those doing the performing but also to those who define the content, aims and objectives, as well as those who evaluate that performance. The system level officials, board members, superintendent, directors, supervisors, and principals all have a stake in examining what they contribute to the problem and its solution (see Griffin, 1983, p. 234).

Traditional staff development has left school system officials, school structure, and school rules unscathed. Because school system officials are usually the ones defining the goals of the organization to which staff development is then directed, the efficacy of school system performance is rarely questioned (see Dobson, Dobson, and Kessinger, 1980, pp. 1–20).

A point of view regarding organizational effectiveness that lays open the traditional sequence of administrative activity in defining and articulating organizational goals and objectives is beginning to emerge (Weick, 1985).

That point of view contradicts much of what is believed to be sound managerial practice. It postulates that goals are established after action, rather than before and that this procedure is normal, rather than abnormal. If so, the practice of improving performance by dealing with teachers first, instead of second, is very logical rather than radical.

Finally, the focus of developmental activities is the whole teacher and not just behavioral manifestations or traces exhibited by the teacher. Performance is more than measurement, it is confronting all of the forces that contribute to moving, shaping, and changing human behavior in human organizations. It is human development.

INQUIRY

Questions and Answers About Chapter One

Question #1: *Why do you talk so much about staff development when the book is about career stages?*

Answer: Because the traditional context of staff development is so pervasive, it is hard to think about the career stages in any other light than the usual "top down" approach. In other words, our pet solution prevents us from re-thinking the problem and arriving at a more satisfactory solution.

Question #2: *How did you arrive at placing so much emphasis on contextual variables in determining the career stages?*

Answer: Because what I saw teachers doing and feeling after being in the school system was different than what I saw them believing and doing prior to their tenure in a system. Therefore, I came to the conclusion that teachers were responding to their work environment in ways they did not always understand, but which ultimately had to be understandable.

Question #3: *How does your criticism of schools differ from those writers of the sixties whom you call "romantic?"*

Answer: I'm not advocating the abolition of school or schooling. I advocate changing a point of view about schooling and particularly the reference point in improving teacher performance. That reference point would change the usual sequence of thinking about what teachers ought to do.

Question #4: *Aren't some of the changes that are happening to teachers out of the system's control?*

Answer: Yes, of course. There are personal situations that do not originate in the work environment, such as a teacher who is bitter because she never married, or a man who feels empty and lost because of a divorce. On the other hand, I argue that we must know about them if we are to truly deal with system activities that will improve teacher performance. That means knowing the whole teacher.

Question #5: *Are you opposed to behavioral objectives or objectives at all?*

Answer: No. I believe that objectives mislead and misinform school people when they deceive them into looking only at behavior and not at the total person who is manifesting the behavior. Some behavior is deceptive. Other behavior looks simple, but masks complex thoughts and motives. Behaviorism has duped us into believing we can solve problems by dealing only with symptoms. When the school system is defining such objectives and the problems are inherent in the system and not in teacher performance, then we have been tricked by our own mental regimentation. Some teacher resistance to system initiatives is healthy. Yet invariably, school officials view almost all teacher resistance as deviant and abnormal. Behaviorism has contributed to this dilemma by negating the question of human will and decision making to mere stimulus-response description. What I want, is to put people back into behavioral questions by placing them first, rather than second.

Question #6: *Aren't there some career ladder plans that incorporate job motivators?*

Answer: To the extent that they include recognition for achievement and thus visibility, that is true. To the extent that they fail to differentiate among intrinsic motivators or recognize where teachers really are in their own thinking, it would not be the case. Some career ladders simply pay teachers more for administration or supervision or extra time on the job. Neither will it help teaching as a profession, nor will it lead to improvement in the overall performance level of the majority of teachers, since the majority don't occupy the upper rungs of any career ladder of which I am aware.

Question #7: *How hard is it to actually move away from the mind-set you describe in this chapter?*

Answer: This may seem like a paradox, but it is very hard and very easy. It is hard, because we have not had any recent practice in it, and most of the legislation of both federal and state branches of government accept and extend narrow behavioristic perspectives. On the other hand, moving away from this perspective is easy, because almost all practitioners have a strong and intuitive grasp of its limitations. After all of the hoopla, our best predictability about performance remains immeasurably crude and limited from the behavioristic perspective. One of the great inhibitors of looking more at the totality of performance is the decline of both precision and predictability. The measurement types are very uncomfortable. Yet, given the best possible precision, they can't account for the largest share of the variance. If one isn't troubled with some ambiguity, there is no problem. Researchers find ambiguity troublesome. Practitioners work with it all the time.

REFERENCES

BELLACK, A., H. Kliebard, R. Hyman, and F. Smith. *The Language of the Classroom.* New York:Teachers College Press (1966).

BIDWELL, C. "The School as a Formal Organization." In *Handbook of Organizations*. J. G. March, ed. Chicago:Rand McNally and Company (1965).

BURDEN, P., ed. *Establishing Career Ladders in Teaching*. Springfield, IL: Charles C. Thomas Publishers (1987).

DOBSON, R., J. Dobson, and J. Kessinger. *Staff Development: A Humanistic Approach*. New York:University Press of America (1980).

ENGLISH, F. *Curriculum Management for Schools, Colleges, Business*. Sprinfield, IL:Charles C. Thomas Publishers (1987).

FISKE, W. "Federal Plan May Put Schools to Test," *The Kentucky Enquirer*. 1, A 4:1 (December, 1987).

GOODMAN, P. *Compulsory Mis-Education*. New York:Vintage Books (1962).

GRIFFIN, G. "Toward a Conceptual Framework for Staff Development." In *Staff Development*, G. Griffin, ed. Chicago:University of Chicago Press (1983).

HERZBERG, F. *Work and the Nature of Man*. New York:World (1966).

KOHL, H. *The Open Classroom* (1974).

KUHN, T. *The Structure of Scientific Revolutions*. Chicago:University of Chicago Press (1962).

LORTIE, D. *School Teacher*. Chicago:University of Chicago Press (1975).

REBORE, R. *Personnel Administration in Education*. Englewood Cliffs, New Jersey:Prentice-Hall (1982).

WEICK, K. "Sources of Order in Underorganized Systems: Themes in Recent Organizational Theory." In *Organizational Theory and Inquiry*. Y. S. Lincoln, ed. Beverly Hills:SAGE Publications (1985).

chapter
=========
TWO

The Teacher Career Stages Model

ESSENTIAL ELEMENTS OF THE MODEL

THE teacher career stages model presented here is a human development model. It is based on the assumption that people are basically good, that they self-actualize (Maslow, 1954), and become confident, contributing adults through the work environment. The relationship between the teacher and his/her immediate superior is crucial to the success of the organization and central to the attainment of the model's objective. That objective is the development of an organization which supports teachers in their efforts to become and remain expert/master teachers.

The model includes five career stages. Most of the recent models of teacher career stages are based on age. While these models contain many worthwhile ideas and are certainly a quantum leap beyond treating all teachers the same, there is a deterministic quality attached to them. These models offer little hope for self-actualization through a teacher's work if she happens to be a teacher who has reached a certain age and made a career decision to stay in the classroom for her entire professional career.

The present model is based on attitude, although there is an overlay of the age component. The five teacher career stages are: anticipatory, expert/master teacher, renewal, withdrawal and exit. The first and last deal with entry and exit from the organization respectively. The other three deal with the attitude and competence of the teacher during those many years in between.

ANTICIPATORY CAREER STAGE

The anticipatory teacher is operationally defined as a non-tenured teacher, and since most states require three years of successful teaching before granting tenure, the anticipatory stage can last that long. Anticipatory teachers can be certified teachers or newly hired teachers with previous experience. For the newly certified teacher, this is the first teaching assignment since graduation. The newly hired teacher is one who has been employed in a teaching position in another district. The newly certified teacher will probably require the full three years before she can be categorized in a different stage, whereas the newly hired teacher can be expected to move out of the anticipatory stage rather quickly. Some of the characteristics of this stage for classroom teachers are the following.

Idealism

Anticipatory teachers are the most idealistic, especially the newly certified ones. After all, they have been studying for four years for the opportunity to stand in front of a class of children and be called a teacher. Being hired for this new job means attaining a goal, set years earlier, for which they have struggled long and hard.

These anticipatory teachers did not choose the teaching profession in order to make a great deal of money, but to gain a degree of immortality by contributing to the education of the nation's most valuable resource, its children. They come into the profession believing they can make a difference in the lives of their students, and of course, they can.

Their preparation has included the study of child development, learning theory, the history of education, pedagogy, and lesson development, as well as practicums and student teaching. They know about behavioral objectives and John Dewey, but they are generally ill-prepared to deal with the pragmatics of day-to-day life as a classroom teacher. Often, they truly believe that the class will finish an assignment in unison and wait patiently for the next.

They have read many of the national reports condemming educators, and they believe they have the skills to change all of that. All are certain that they will be able to ignite the fire of the desire to learn in each of their students. They know because they care, and they are dedicated to working hard.

Boundless Energy

Anticipatory teachers are filled with boundless energy; a sixty-hour week is not unusual for them. After a position is secured, it is not uncommon for these teachers to send away for every freebie they can find. They scour professional journals for ideas. They give up their evenings and weekends to make materials for individualized lessons. They volunteer for committees, take on coaching responsibilities, and provide extra help for their students. They arrive early and stay late. These are the teachers who drive custodians crazy in the summer when they attempt to get into their rooms, before the wax on the floor is dry, to decorate for the next year's session.

Open to New Ideas

Fresh from their higher education experience, the anticipatory teachers are open to any new idea. For the previous four years as an undergraduate, they encountered many new ideas. Rarely are they heard to say, "It won't work!" or "We tried that before!" or "I already do that!" If they can be faulted for their openness, it is because they often try too many new ideas. They tend to accept everything they read and sometimes fail to put it into their present context.

Creativity

Creativity is operationally defined for the anticipatory teacher as the ability and willingness not to be bound by the teacher's manual. Anticipatory teachers freely embellish, modify, and create new activities to supplement, improve, and enhance those suggested by the textbook publishers. They are often prompted to modify the lessons based on what they perceive to be the needs of the students.

These teachers often freely seek teaming relationships with other content area teachers in an effort to develop an integrated approach to instruction. A suggestion in a teacher's manual can quickly turn into a play, a major production, or an elaborate culminating activity. When faced with limiting resources, these teachers will aggressively seek donations from stores, businesses, or parents. The attics, garages, and basements of friends and relatives often become a hunting ground for instructional materials.

This is not to suggest that creativity is not found in the other career stages. However, in the anticipatory stage it seems to flow more continuously through the design and implementation of lessons. Many times though, the creative endeavors, while highly motivational, fail to meet the intended instructional objective. That aside, it is a strong positive force burning brightly in the anticipatory teacher.

Growth Orientation

Anticipatory teachers are anxious to learn. Realizing that most of what they know about teaching has been learned from books, they are like dry sponges waiting to soak up the pragmatics of making it all work in classrooms. Their minds are open and they actively seek out opportunities to grow. If the district offers in-service courses, they often take advantage of them. They listen and sometimes even take notes at faculty meetings and staff development sessions. They like to engage other teachers in discussions about what works. Very quickly, these teachers learn about their own deficiencies as effective classroom teachers. Problems with classroom management, lesson pacing, student assessment, and lesson design to accommodate learning levels and styles quickly descend (see Keefe, 1987).

EXPERT/MASTER CAREER STAGE

Before tenure is granted, the anticipatory teacher should be operating at the expert/master teacher level or at least be showing all the signs necessary for the district to be assured that this is a teacher who has the skills, knowledge, and attitudes to be classified in that career stage for many years to come. To expect less is to acknowledge that the district is content with less than expert/master teachers; or, worse yet, it suggests that the administrative staff lacks the necessary skills to transform anticipatory teachers into expert/master teachers.

The label for this career stage was chosen carefully. To call it Master Teacher Career Stages does not quite relate the high level of instructional effectiveness required of teachers at this career stage. David Berliner (October, 1986) classified teachers as novice, good, or expert. He noted that expert teachers process several sources of information simultaneously, seem to know instinctively when the classroom is out of sinc, and immediately make it clear to students that they, not the students, are in charge of the classroom. In addition, expert/master teachers have high expectations for student performance of district mandated curriculum and effective time management routines. Expert/master teachers are the superstars of our profession.

Control

Without a doubt, the expert/master teacher is in control of the classroom. One senses the order the minute one walks into the room. Children can be involved in a variety of activities, but there is little off-task behavior (see Flanders, 1965). Materials are readily available to the students and easily accessible. Students finishing activities at varying times know what to do next. Whether the teacher is providing individual instruction to one student, assisting a small group, or directing a total class discussion, she has the attention of the student(s) when she is teaching. Learning is going on.

The anticipatory teacher viewing this kind of classroom often cannot see what the teacher is doing to achieve the positive classroom climate. Even the expert/master teacher is often hard pressed to explain what she does to make it work so well. One of the keys to her success lies in what the teacher does during the first week of school. It is at this time that the expert/master teacher establishes herself as "in control" of the class. She does this through the establishment of procedures. Children learn quickly what they are expected to do in this room and they perform accordingly. It is often worth the price of a substitute teacher to allow an anticipatory teacher to spend a day visiting the classrooms of expert/master teachers to observe this phenomenon.

Self-Actualization

The expert/master teacher self-actualizes through her job. Her feelings of positive worth as a professional come from her daily activities in the classroom. This inner feeling flowing through her veins is the reason she entered the profession, and the glue that keeps her there year after year. Maslow (1954) defined self-actualization as the need to fulfill one's potential. He placed it at the top of his hierarchy, above the need for self-esteem. According to Maslow's theory, the self-actualizing expert/master teacher will actively seek responsibility and work hard to achieve success. In the school environment, achieving success for the teacher means achieving success for the students. The intrinsic rewards of teaching are the fuel for the expert/master teacher's self-actualization.

With-it-ness

The expert/master teacher has often been accused of having eyes in the back of her head. "With-it-ness" refers to the ability of the expert/master teacher to be able to scan the entire classroom with all of the senses: sight, sound, smell, touch, and taste and know when something is out of order—to know what it is and how to correct it. Expert/master teachers are "with-it." Carried around in her head is a set of patterns of what should be in the classroom at any given time (Yinger, 1987). These patterns, developed over a period of time, are based on experience. In studies conducted by Berliner (1986), anticipatory teachers and expert/master teachers were shown pictures of classrooms. Typically, the anticipatory teacher would focus on one group, one activity or one thing, whereas the expert/master teacher would see the classroom as a whole and could describe many activities, students, and things after one brief scan of the picture. The expert/master teacher could also quickly identify what is out of order in the classroom.

With-it-ness has been described as an expert/master teacher's sixth sense.

Evolving

You have heard the saying, "You are either getting better or you're getting worse." Nothing remains static. This is equally true both for the expert/master teacher and the anticipatory teacher. The expert/master teacher is continually evolving, getting better, but when that process stops, and the teacher begins to move in a different direction, he/she begins to slip into another career stage.

One can always count on the expert/master teachers to be interested in new ideas. When the Madeline Hunter movement began to sweep the country, the expert/master teachers made it the success it has been. These expert/master teachers quickly realized that many of the ideas expressed in the direct instruction model were ones they had already incorporated into their teaching. The model provided legitimacy for what they were already doing. Because of the numbers of expert/master teachers, and because of most teachers' natural instinct to want to improve, the model has been embraced by large numbers of teachers. If the model had been unacceptable to the expert/master teacher, all of the administrative mandates in the world wouldn't have made it the success it is.

It became so successful because it fit into the internal "becoming" mechanism of the individual teacher. Nothing more, nothing less. It provided positive reinforcement for the exemplary practices already in place, and provided improvement for other, less polished, but valued skills. It was a case of an individual teacher deciding on what is worthwhile for her, it was not the discovery of the "recipe" for effective teaching.

WITHDRAWAL CAREER STAGE

The term withdrawal carries with it a negative connotation. I've chosen it purposely to emphasize the need for administrative intervention for teachers at this career stage. The type of intervention required depends on the level of withdrawal. This career stage has three sub-stages: initial withdrawal, persistent withdrawal, and deep withdrawal.

Initial Withdrawal

The teacher at the early withdrawal career stage is one who would be referred to as okay. This teacher is in limbo. If the principal were asked to list the top three and bottom three teachers in the building, this teacher's name would not appear. Teachers at this career stage are the most neglected in the system, and they may be the most numerous as well.

Adequate

A teacher at the initial withdrawal stage performs her job satisfactorily. While there may be deficiencies in skill level, they are not dramatic enough to cause the administrator to focus attention on correcting them. Student performance is average for these teachers. There is little innovation in the classroom. The lesson plans used last year, are often used again and again. These teachers rarely request permission to attend workshops or conferences. They are dependable, predictable, solid, and stable, and can be dull, unimaginative, and steadfast in their beliefs.

Quiet

In a crowded teacher's room, the teacher in initial withdrawal likes being part of the the group, but generally is not recognized as the group leader. These teachers tend to keep their opinions to themselves, voicing them only when they are pressed or asked in a direct question.

Attendance patterns, arrival and departure time, interaction with parents, grading practices, classroom management, and lesson design of the teacher in initial withdrawal are topics which generate little conversation within the community, among other teachers, or between the teacher and the administrator. The teacher in early withdrawal rarely files a grievance or asks for exceptions to the contract. When new committees are being formed, this teacher rarely volunteers. When innovative programs are being piloted, this teacher stays away. When criticism is being voiced, she remains on the sidelines. This teacher can be unnoticeable because he/she is quiet.

Follower

Once a position has been taken, a program piloted, or a model adopted, the teacher in initial withdrawal will quietly follow along. Whatever the issue, this teacher tends to go along with the majority. An administrator who would interpret the quiet position of a teacher at this stage as support, is often surprised to see this teacher along with a group of more vocal teachers protesting some administrative decision.

It is often difficult to determine the real position of these teachers since they do tend to follow the crowd. They frequently follow others because they have no position of their own. To them, "It really doesn't matter!"

Responsive

The teacher in initial withdrawal is particularly receptive to encouragement. Left alone, she would tend not to initiate any new behavior, but given the support and encouragement of a caring administrator, this teacher will respond quickly. Teachers in initial withdrawal can be turned around and become motivated to develop into expert/master teachers. However, they will generally not initiate this action on their own. Left alone, their inertia will continue until they eventually slip into the next level of withdrawal.

Persistent Withdrawal

This is the career stage most often associated with the burned-out teacher, who is also, generally, the most vocally negative teacher in the system.

Critical

Teachers at the career stage of persistent withdrawal are critical of the system, the board, the administration, the parents, the community, and the students. On occasion, they are even critical of other teachers, especially those who received recognition for some outstanding contribution to the system. In extreme cases, if the number of teachers in the symptomatic withdrawal career stage is large, the expert/master teachers in the system will tend to want to hide their competence because of the criticism they receive from this group.

Teachers in this career stage diligently watch the move of every administrator. Immediately upon identifying a mistake, they take great delight in pointing it out, dissecting it, and proclaiming it to the world from their podium in the teacher's room. Those well connected with board members take great satisfaction in reporting it in detail to the board as another example of the incompetency of the district's administration.

Unresponsive

Teachers in persistent withdrawal dogmatically resist change and label it as bad, dehumanizing, and disruptive to the system. They are generally unresponsive to a suggestion made by the administration. They not only refuse to volunteer for any committee to improve anything, but they are critical of the outcome of its work. One of their favorite expressions is, "I've seen superintendents come and superintendents go, and I'll be here long after you have gone." Unfortunately, the statement is often true. Teachers in persistent withdrawal tend to stay in the system long after they have ceased to be productive, contributing professionals. When you hear the comment, "He has retired on the job," the teacher being described is one in persistent withdrawal.

Obstructionist

The teacher in persistent withdrawal can sometimes be an obstructionist. Fortunately, the number of teachers in this category is so small, they tend to be almost nonexistent. But almost every school system has one or two of them. Unless the administration recognizes the career stage they are in and takes steps to intervene, they can sap the creativity and energy from the system. Since they are vocal, they attract attention. Administrators tend to react to them. Board members are aware of what they say. Sometimes their impact on the system is greatly exaggerated simply because we respond to them. Too often, our reactions to them permit them to be obstructionists.

Psycho-Social Problem

Many teachers in persistent withdrawal exhibit various levels of psycho-social problems. They have difficulty getting along with other people. They often tend to be loners, or at the other extreme, incessant talkers. Their relationship with their families can also be strained. Sometimes these people live alone. Their entire world revolves around their activities at school. For some, their home life presents so many problems over which they have no control, that they live their lives through their job. Their feelings of self-worth come not from doing a good job, but from being the self-appointed watchdog of the district.

For the most part, these people are looking for help. They have been unable to solve their problems, and blame the system for not helping them. While it is possible to bring a teacher out of this career stage, the process is long and time-consuming. The administrator attempting the career stage transformation needs to be fully aware of the time and energy required to complete it.

Deep Withdrawal

Few districts have teachers in this career stage. For the teacher in deep withdrawal, the possibility of rebirth, of moving out of withdrawal and into the area of expert/master teacher is very slim. The only solution for the teacher in this career stage, is to exit the system for another career or to retire.

Deficient

The teacher in deep withdrawal is visibly incompetent. The skill deficiency is so great in so many areas, that it would be nearly impossible to re-train this teacher. In reality, the teacher probably never had the skills of an expert/master teacher to begin with. By any measure, this is a person who, by her very presence in the classroom, is probably harmful to students, and cannot be tolerated in the classroom.

Defensive

Teachers in deep withdrawal do not see their own deficiencies. They would not label themselves as such. Any hint of a deficiency, either verbal or written, always generates a rebuttal. Someone else is always to blame, the observation instrument, the subjective view of the administrator, the deficiencies of the students. Never the teacher.

Difficult

Because of the defensive nature of these teachers and the extent of the skill deficiency, these are the most difficult teachers to deal with. Early retirement, a career change, or a "buy out" are normally the best solutions. Removing tenure is an option, but one that the district should choose with its eyes wide open. Even the most incompetent teacher has friends. And after all, if the district would attempt to remove tenure from one teacher, then every teacher in the system would feel vulnerable. As an administrator, do not expect to be rewarded for your attempts to rid the system of incompetent teachers. Even a board of education who has initially encouraged such efforts, begins to lose heart when the student, staff, and parent supporters of the teacher begin to show up at board meetings.

Implementing a human development model based on the career stages concept prevents teachers from reaching this career stage. No district knowingly hires a teacher at any level of withdrawal. If the system has teachers at this level, it happened while the teacher was employed by the district. The system, the board, the administration, the staff, and the teacher must take responsibility for allowing it to happen.

RENEWAL CAREER STAGE

Teachers in renewal are getting better, not worse, and are involved in some growth activity designed to lead them to the expert/master teacher stage. Perhaps not all will make it to that stage, but they are attempting to get there through their renewal activities. Unfortunately, present staff development activities often fail to address individual teacher renewal. For the renewal to take place, the growth and development activities must be seen as important for the individual teacher. The teacher must be committed to the growth goal. It cannot be prescribed.

Reactivated

Teachers entering this stage are most frequently coming from the early stages of withdrawal. The first one to know a teacher is headed into withdrawal is the teacher himself/herself. They begin to notice that things are different. They are not getting the same satisfaction out of their jobs. They are beginning to feel bored. It can be a frightening experience. They have always thought of themselves as expert/master teachers, and they know in some subtle way, all of that is changing.

Some teachers can put themselves into a state of renewal. Recognizing the early signs, they seek out ways to reactivate themselves. Some will explore a new model of teaching. Some will take a course, attend a conference, or join a professional organization.

Whether activated by themselves or by an administrator, the teacher in renewal is remotivated and re-energized. The characteristics of an anticipatory teacher can be seen again in the teacher in renewal.

Focused Growth

The teacher in renewal is idealistic, full of energy, and is seeking new knowledge. In the case of renewal, the growth area is focused. While the anticipatory teacher is generally excited about most aspects of being a teacher, the teacher in renewal is pursuing growth in a directed area.

Acquiring New Skills

The teacher in renewal is learning how to do things differently, to expand her knowledge base or to develop a new area of competence. Acquiring a new skill is not easy. Blanchard (1986) has identified four steps in acquiring a new skill. The first step is that of the enthusiastic beginner. The teacher is excited about the prospects of what she has decided to learn. Unless supported, this step soon turns into one typified by the disillusioned learner. The task becomes more difficult than the teacher thought, because the information is hard to assimilate. When expert help is needed to overcome an obstacle, it is not necessarily forthcoming. If the assistance is there, the teacher may move to the next critical step, that of the reluctant contributor. The renewal activity will have been a success only when the final step is reached, that of the peak performer.

Dependent

Throughout the process of acquiring a new skill, the teacher is highly dependent. Efforts at renewal must be supported by the school system. One word from a cynical administrator, and all efforts toward renewal can stop. I suspect the number of teachers in a system who are in the first two levels of withdrawal can be directly traced to the lack of support from the system for attempts at renewal. Once rejected in an attempt at renewal, a teacher may try once more, but if it happens again, it is not likely that the teacher would attempt a third effort toward renewal.

EXIT CAREER STAGE

The teacher at the exit stage is about to leave the system. She may wish to leave because teaching wasn't the right career in the first place. Some leave to pursue a second career. Unfortunately, some of these are the profession's brightest and best.

Take the case of Krista Ramsey. For eight years she taught English at a small high school near Akron, Ohio. She says she didn't quit because of money, accountability, or the increased "social work" responsibilities of the job. She quit because she realized that the pressures of teaching left her too little time to spend with her students, the primary reason she entered teaching.

Ramsey provided an example. A student came by her office but she was involved in curriculum development. Again the student came by, and Ramsey was involved in a department conference. She never saw the student after that. She later learned that the student, Linda, was pregnant. She was only fifteen years old. "I had gone into teaching to help kids, but I had been too busy with meetings and course outlines and fund raising to help this one" (Ramsey, 1987, August 30, B-3). Ramsey ponders on this problem ". . . I wonder if we as a society haven't put so many demands on our teachers that we've left them with precious little time to really care about our children" (B-3). Ramsey isn't alone. Each year in Ohio, approximately 1,727 public school teachers start their teaching careers. At the end of the year, about one-fourth leave the profession (Ramsey, 1987, August 30, B). Whatever the reasons, before the exit takes place, most teachers exhibit attitudinal and behavioral changes.

Commitment Shift

No matter whether the teacher enters the exit stage from the anticipatory stage, the expert/master teacher stage, or the withdrawal stage, once the decision to leave the school system has been reached, the teacher's commitment to the district changes.

The teacher begins to focus her creative energy on plans to be accomplished after she leaves. She is no longer committed to the district in the same way, because soon she will no longer be a part of the system.

Plans to improve her teaching skills are of little interest to her; plans to prepare for her life after teaching are of great interest.

Nostalgia

Teachers about to leave the system are often nostalgic about their years of service to the system. Changes within the system are remembered and discussed. Depending on the career stage prior to exit, these reminiscences can be positive or negative. It is important for the teacher about to leave the system to carry away with her positive memories of her years of service.

Need for Recognition

There is a strong need by teachers to be recognized for their contributions. Failure of the system to acknowledge the contributions they have made will cause them and others who are about to exit, to become cynical.

For those who have invested more than twenty years of their professional life in the system, the need for recognition is especially strong. They need a little slice of immortality from the system. They need to know that the countless hours of dedicated service were noted and appreciated.

Judgmental

When they leave the system, teachers have some definite ideas about its strengths and weaknesses. Based on their years of service, they feel positive or negative about the system and have a strong desire to express these feelings.

The exit stage is one which administrators tend to ignore. Such lack of attention is a mistake, because the exit stage offers administrators an opportunity to show to the entire staff that the human being and her commitment are valued by the organization.

SUMMARY

Edwin Bridges (1986) has predicted that approximately one million teachers will be hired in the United States between 1986 and 1990. Each of these teachers is expected to become an expert. But will they? If the past is repeated, these teachers will vary greatly in their level of competence five to ten years after they are hired. Why? Part of the answer lies in the relationship between the needs of the teacher and how these needs are met through the formal teacher-administrator relationship.

A recent ad by Merrill Lynch stated, "With vision, your world knows no boundaries." Applied to the context of expectations for teacher competence, it implies that it is possible for each one of those one million teachers to indeed become masters at their trade. Applied to the present teaching cadre, it means that our present teaching staff could all become master teachers.

This expectation may be idealistic, but it is the expectation which leads to the development of the career stages model described in this book. Someone long ago described an educator as one with his head in the clouds and his feet on the ground. The "head in the clouds" part can be applied to the idealistic notion that all professional staff people in schools could be classified as master teachers. The "feet on the ground" part is based on the reality that not all teachers are good. A few are even incompetent. While educators readily agree that all teachers are not at the master level, the public image of the professional educator is sometimes a negative one because of the incompetent few.

If you accept the image frequently portrayed in the press, teachers are burned out, demoralized, and lacking in basic skills. The fact of the matter is that vast differences exist in the quality of the country's professional educators. This is not a new phenomenon. Perhaps it has been accentuated in recent years, because teachers tend to teach longer, and many stay with the same district for most of their professional careers. When teaching jobs were plentiful and student enrollment was increasing, new teachers were continually being hired. Fresh ideas were coming into a district by the very nature of the job market. Because of this movement in personnel, the less competent teacher was not so visible.

For the past decade, however, many school districts have been faced with declining enrollment. Teachers have tended not to move from one district to another for fear of losing their seniority and making themselves vulnerable to riffing. Today it is not unusual to find a district where the average years of service in the district are fifteen to eighteen and the average age of the staff is in the early fifties.

While many master teachers can be found among these veterans, the number who would be labeled with other descriptions is large. Traditional staff development programs will not improve this situation. It may be improved through a carefully planned human development program built on the career stages model.

The term human development is appearing more frequently in professional literature today. I like to think of it as typifying a new paradigm (Kuhn, 1962) in which administrators interact with and help to improve professional staff.

If one reviewed the professional literature of the early 1900s, the term human development would rarely be found. The term most often used at that time in articles dealing with the improvement of staff was supervision. Administrators were charged with the responsibility of ensuring that teachers were doing their job. Between 1930 and 1960, much of the literature on staff development dealt with in-service. Teachers were staying at their jobs longer. It was no longer necessary for a woman to quit her job if she married. A few women were even attempting to balance parenting and full-time employment. In-service programs were designed to provide teachers with new skills. These programs were usually short-term and content specific.

In the early 1960s and continuing until the early 1980s, the terminology in vogue was staff development. The implication with the change in terminology was that a staff development program extended over a longer period of time and involved an entire faculty. Administrators frequently designed full-year staff development programs or even multi-year staff development programs. Whatever the program design, the entire staff usually received it. During this same period of time, unions became more and more powerful. Staff development days, which were not valued by the teaching staff, were frequently negotiated out of the contract.

The generic model for staff development includes conducting a needs assessment, developing goals and objectives, and designing, implementing, and evaluating the program. The problem with this model (as noted in chapter 1) is that it treats all staff members the same. It is based on the assumption that if the majority of teachers desire a certain type of in-service program, then the entire staff would benefit from it. The fallacies of this approach were explained in the previous chapter. Few districts can afford more than three days of contact time for the entire professional staff. In this short time, it is expected that the staff will get off to a "motivational start" for a new academic year: new skills are taught, high morale is built and maintained, and necessary information is shared with the staff. In addition, typical staff development activities deal with the formal needs of the organization and the formal behavior of staff and administrators. Human development models take into account both the formal and the informal needs of the staff and the administrators. There is acceptance of the assumption that how an individual feels about him- or herself affects how that individual functions within the organization. These models deal with the wellness of the total organization, the organizational climate (Stern, 1970), and the ability of the organization to set a mission, and work with vision towards accomplishing it.

As we move from a period of staff development to the new paradigm of human development, we are moving to the design of organizational improvement models which impact not only in-service or staff development, but also include both formal and informal interactive activities in the organization (see Dillion-Peterson, 1981). Human development activities can be synthesizing to the organization, creating a synergy which can dramatically transform the work environment and vastly improve the number of master teachers in the organization.

The teacher career stages model presented in this chapter identifies five teacher career stages. The anticipatory and exit stages are defined by a teacher's entrance into or exit from the system. The other three stages, expert/master, withdrawal, and renewal, depend on the internal motivation and competence level of the teacher. The individual factors in turn, are stimulated by the teacher's working conditions.

A theoretical view of the career stages model is shown in Figure 1.

A teacher entering the system was moved from anticipatory to expert/master teacher to renewal to expert/master teacher—and finally to exit the system. With appropriate administrative support and intervention, I hope that this is the cycle which will be followed.

Unfortunately, some teachers enter at the anticipatory stage, go to withdrawal, and finally exit. Some enter at the anticipatory stage and exit. The somewhat depressing cycle is one of entering at the an-

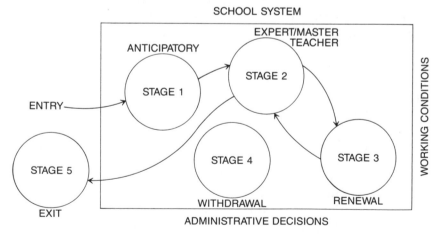

FIGURE 1. A theoretical view of the career stages model of classroom teaching.

ticipatory stage, going to withdrawal, and not exiting the system. Preventing this cycle is why this book has been written.

The ideal is represented in Figure 1. A continual cycle of renewal–expert/master teacher–renewal–expert/master teacher–for the teacher's entire professional life.

INQUIRY

Questions and Answers About Chapter Two

Question #1: *You seem to indicate that the career stages model is based on the internal conditions of a teacher, yet the first stage is a legal category imposed externally. Isn't this a contradiction in the model?*

Answer: I don't think so. While the model states that all teachers enter the system at the anticipatory stage, it also states that they move out of that stage based on their internal conditions and demonstrated competence. An experienced teacher may enter the system at the anticipatory stage, but move to the expert/master teacher stage by the end of the fourth month.

Question #2: *The model you present begins with the anticipatory teacher and moves to the expert/master teacher. Isn't there any room between, or does your experience suggest that this is a clean-cut division?*

Answer: It is idealistic to assume that all anticipatory teachers move directly to the expert/master teacher stage. Those who are striving to reach the expert/ master teacher level are in a stage of renewal. Those who have stopped trying to get there, and who are content to be average, are really in the early stages of withdrawal.

Question #3: *The model suggests that what teachers do is a combination of what's inside and the interaction with system variables such as working conditions and administrative decisions. What precedents are there for this model in organizational life?*

Answer: Probably the most explicit was the work of psychologist Henry Murray in his 1938 book *Explorations in Personality*. Murray identified two kinds of external social presses on a person. These were the control press, which was a pattern of social forces that inhibited a person's growth needs, and the development press, which was a pattern that fostered growth needs. Murray developed thirty dimensions or factors of personality and environment. They included such things as change, energy, play, ego achievement, and harm avoidance. When scored and summed, the result produced an Organizational Climate Index or OCI. Many of my ideas are quite similar to Murray's, although when I developed the career stages model, I didn't have Murray in mind.

REFERENCES

BERLINER, D. "On the Expert Teacher: A Conversation with David Berliner," *Educational Leadership*, 44(2): 4–9 (October 1986).

BRIDGES, E. M. *The Incompetent Teacher*. Philadelphia:Falmer Press (1986).

DILLION-PETERSON, B. *Staff Development/Organization Development*. Alexandria, VA:Association for Supervision and Curriculum Development (1981).

FLANDERS, N. A. *Teacher Influence, Pupil Attitudes, and Achievement*. Washington, DC:Government Printing Office (1965).

KEEFE, J. W. *Learning Style Theory and Practice*. Reston, VA:National Association of Secondary School Principals (1987).

KUHN, T. *The Structure of Scientific Revolutions*. Chicago, IL:University of Chicago Press (1962).

MASLOW, A. *Motivation and Personality*. New York:Harper and Row (1954).

MURRAY, H. *Explorations in Personality*. New York:Oxford University Press (1938).

RAMSEY, K. "The Spark to Continue Burns Out," *Cincinnati Enquirer* (B) (August 1987).

STERN, C. G. "The Measurement of Psychological Characteristics of Students and Learning Environments." In *Measurement in Personality and Cognition*. S. J. Messick and J. Ross, eds. New York:Wiley (1962).

YINGER, R. "Learning the Language of Practice," *Curriculum Inquiry*, 17(3): 293–318 (1987).

chapter
THREE

The Anticipatory Stage

THE LAMP OF IDEALISM

THE superintendent has just finished interviewing a candidate for a social studies teaching position. She is quietly shaking her head, smiling, and reflecting on the interview. The candidate had recently completed her undergraduate training at the local state university and was filled with enthusiasm, eager for the opportunity to put into practice all the new and creative ideas she had learned.

She had displayed a thorough knowledge of Dewey, Bloom, Erickson, Taba, and Piaget in the interview and could describe the Madeline Hunter direct instruction model in detail. She knew about Mager type behavioral objectives and had even attempted to include them in the four-week instructional unit she had developed on Twentieth Century Indians. There were no signs of burnout, and she didn't even ask for a copy of the teacher's contract: she was a teacher at the anticipatory stage.

The superintendent smiled because she had been reminded of her own feelings at this career stage.

CHARACTERISTICS OF FUTURE ANTICIPATORY TEACHERS

The anticipatory teacher of the future will be different from the anticipatory teacher of the past. That fact is soundly underscored by an examination of some of the changes in certification required by the reforms of the eighties. The impact of these reforms has been summarized on the following pages. In 1988, at least 64 percent of the fifty states changed their initial certification requirements. These changes primarily reflect the mandate to pass the National

A Summary of Changes in Teacher Preparation in the Fifty States—1988.*

Types of Changes

State	Certification Initial	Certification Alternative	Curriculum Teacher Ed.	Admission Standards	Incentives to Enter Teaching as a Career
Alabama		yes			
Alaska	yes				
Arizona		yes		yes	
Arkansas			yes	yes	
California		yes	yes		
Colorado			yes	yes (1990)	State scolarships for outstanding teacher ed. students
Connecticut	yes (1990)	yes	yes (1992)		
Delaware		yes			State/local programs to encourage minority students
D.C.				yes	Scholarships for outstanding teacher education majors
Florida	yes		yes		
Georgia					
Hawaii					
Idaho	yes				

A Summary of Changes in Teacher Preparation in the Fifty States—1988* (continued).

Types of Changes

State	Certification Initial	Certification Alternative	Curriculum Teacher Ed.	Admission Standards	Incentives to Enter Teaching as a Career
Illinois	yes		yes (1991)	yes	State scholarships for subject areas in short supply
Indiana	yes				State scholarships for minority students entering teaching
Iowa			yes	yes	State scholarships for teachers of math and science
Kansas	yes			yes	
Kentucky	yes		yes	yes	
Louisiana					
Maine	yes		yes		
Maryland	yes				State funds to minority colleges
Massachusetts	yes		yes (1989)		
Michigan	yes (1989)		yes		
Minnesota	yes		yes (1989)		
Mississippi	yes	yes	yes	yes	
Missouri	yes (1990)		yes	yes	State loans for students entering teaching

41

A Summary of Changes in Teacher Preparation in the Fifty States—1988* (continued).

Types of Changes

State	Certification Initial	Certification Alternative	Curriculum Teacher Ed.	Admission Standards	Incentives to Enter Teaching as a Career
Montana	yes			yes	
Nebraska	yes (1989)			yes	
Nevada	yes (1989)			yes	
New Hampshire	yes		yes	yes	
New Jersey	yes	yes			State loans for outstanding students entering teaching
New Mexico		yes	yes		
New York					State loans for oustanding students entering teaching
North Carolina			yes (1990)	yes	
North Dakota	yes		yes	yes	
Ohio	yes (1991)		yes	yes	State loans for teachers in geographic/content poor supply
Oklahoma	yes	yes	yes	yes	
Oregon	yes (1989)		yes (1990)		State loans to minority students/areas of short supply
Pennsylvania	yes		yes		

A Summary of Changes in Teacher Preparation in the Fifty States—1988* (continued).

State	Certification Initial	Certification Alternative	Curriculum Teacher Ed.	Admission Standards	Types of Changes Incentives to Enter Teaching as a Career
Rhode Island	yes				
South Carolina	yes	yes	yes	yes	
South Dakota			yes		
Tennessee			yes (1990)	yes	
Texas	yes	yes	yes (1991)		
Utah			yes (1989)	yes (1989)	
Vermont			yes (1989)	yes	
Virginia	yes		yes (1990)		
Washington	yes (1993)		yes (1993)	yes	
West Virginia	yes	yes		yes	
Wisconsin	yes		yes	yes (1989)	
Wyoming			yes	yes	
Totals	32 (64%)	12 (24%)	32 (64%)	26 (52%)	

*Data extrapolated from C. Leatherman, "Reforms in Education of Schoolteachers Face Tough New Challenges," Chronicle of Higher Education, 34, p. 1, A30–36 (April 20, 1988).

Note: Dates in parentheses indicate year change is to take effect. States with no changes may have passed laws in 1986 but are not shown on this chart.

43

Teachers Exam or some kind of state-developed test (Leatherman, 1988).

Another 64 percent of the states have changed their teacher preparation curriculum, which now requires more subject content preparation than before. Fifty-two percent of the states have altered their certification requirements to stipulate a higher undergraduate grade point average or test score specifications. The data also indicate that almost one-fourth of the states have established an alternative certification channel for people already in possession of a bachelor's degree to become teachers.

These new requirements imply that the anticipatory teacher of tomorrow will have higher test scores and a longer preparation period in a content area than was typically true before these new mandates were passed. Whether they produce better teachers remains to be seen.

The adjective that best describes a teacher at the anticipatory career stage is effervescent. The anticipatory teacher is excited about almost everything: the school, the materials, the other teachers, the curriculum, and most of all the students. The teacher at this stage, more than at any other stage, is filled with a passion for teaching.

These teachers believe they can solve all of the problems of education, motivate all of the youngsters, individualize the instruction to meet the learning needs of every student, and become recognized as an expert/master teacher with a few years of experience.

Once teachers at the anticipatory stage get jobs, they immediately begin to collect materials and often scour the professional journals for freebies. Their cars and their homes or apartments soon begin to overflow with materials. They often try to enter the school building as soon as their contract has been signed, in order to decorate the bulletin boards or rearrange the furniture in the classroom. It has been reported that on occasion during the summer, a teacher at the anticipatory stage has even attempted to climb into her classroom through the window.

While teachers at this stage do not lack motivation, they are decidedly naive about the realities of the classroom teacher's responsibilities. Even though they have typically completed nine to twelve weeks of student teaching, there is a quantum leap between teaching selected lessons with the regular classroom teacher close by and being completely in charge of the educational growth and development of a class of twenty to thirty students with diverse levels of competence, interest, and dedication. The anticipatory teacher quickly realizes that all youngsters do not complete an assignment in unison, and that their level of achievement varies greatly. One commonly accepted measure of the span of achievement in a grade is to take that grade and add one which means that heterogeneously grouped students in an eighth grade class typically have an achievement span of nine years.

Motivation

The key to motivating the anticipatory teacher is to keep the lamp of idealism burning while her skills necessary to becoming an expert/master teacher improve. Whether the teacher is newly trained or an expert/master teacher from another district, she will be at the anticipatory stage until she displays the skills and competency associated with the expert/master teacher.

IN-SERVICE OF ANTICIPATORY TEACHERS

Many states are now requiring districts to develop induction programs. Pennsylvania, for example, mandated that each district submit an induction plan to the Department of Education prior to June 1, 1987. To help districts with this process, the Pennsylvania Association for Supervision and Curriculum Development (1986) prepared a review of the literature which identified five key areas to be addressed in any induction program: psycho-social, educational, managerial, informational, and evaluative. These five areas are worth considering in the design of in-service training, curriculum monitoring, supervisory practices, and reward structures for anticipatory teachers.

Psycho-Social Needs

The psycho-social needs of anticipatory teachers include: support, collegiality, caring, professionalism, and growth (PASCD, p. 22). Entering any new social system heightens a newcomer's anxiety level. These feelings are magnified when the recruit is newly trained. The move from being a student in a classroom, listening to a teacher, to being the teacher is a big step. The new teacher needs to become integrated into the school's social fabric, and this support is most commonly provided through a mentor program. It has been a long-standing practice for principals to select a teacher on the staff to be a new teacher's buddy to show her the ropes. State requirements for induction programs have formalized that practice. When designing a mentor teacher program, it is important that the procedures allow for a good relationship between the mentor teacher and the new teacher.

The anticipatory teacher must quickly become integrated into the decision-making fabric of the school. He or she must recognize that teacher opinions are valued, and that a formal mechanism exists for guaranteeing all teachers the opportunity to provide input when decisions are being made. These procedures not only heighten the feelings of professionalism for the anticipatory teacher, but also improve the decision-making process for the school system (Belasco and Alutto, 1972).

New teachers need to know where to go to get help and support, because feelings of inadequacy are inevitable, since their "teacher self-concept" is brand-new and vulnerable. These anticipatory teachers must know that the district recognizes this psycho-social need and is prepared to assist them. When the psycho-social needs of the anticipatory teacher are met, she is free to concentrate on perfecting her skills and attaining the status of expert/master teacher.

Educational Needs

The educational needs of anticipatory teachers are great and districts should design an in-service program for them that addresses as many of these needs as possible. Educational needs include: first day, curricular content, instructional strategies, materials, student needs, and assessment/evaluation. This list could serve as the topics for a seven-week in-service course to be offered each fall for new teachers. Various administrators in the district might be responsible for teaching the separate sections, which would enable the new teacher to meet many of the administrators in the district, and would permit the administrators to improve their skills as well. The first session of the course should be scheduled to meet before school begins and could be linked to a social event at which the board of education has an opportunity to personally meet the new staff. In districts where the number of new teachers is too large to be accommodated in one in-service training series, several could be offered.

First Day

No day is more important to the success of a school year than the
first day. When the teacher is brand-new to the district, students entering the classroom have no past history on which to base an opinion. It is a critical time for the teacher and the students. Within the
first hour, most of the students in the class decide whether or not
they are going to like the class, and they learn what the expectations
are for performance, how hard they will have to work, what they can
get away with, where the teacher is vulnerable, how discipline will
be handled, and what the class routine will be like. It is imperative
that high standards and high expectations are set from the beginning. As the year goes on, expectations can be lowered, but it is extremely difficult to increase them. An in-service session dealing
with setting the right tone for a productive learning environment
should be held before school begins.

Curricular Content

It is important for new teachers to have a copy of the district's curriculum for the subject they are teaching as soon as they are hired.
Most teachers will ask for a teacher's manual right away, but often
they begin the school year without reviewing the official district curriculum, which tells them what proficiencies the average student is
expected to have after a year of instruction. If it doesn't, it is a poorly
developed document and must be revised. Too often, new teachers
plan to cover the material in the textbook during the year of instruction. However, they should focus on what the students learn, rather
than what is taught. It would be impossible for every student to
master all the knowledge, skills, or attitudes addressed in a textbook
within a given year. A properly developed curriculum guide will provide the answer to the question, "Of all the things you could teach,
what will you teach?" The answer to that question should take into
consideration the amount of available instruction time, the accessible materials and resources, and the students' ability level.

Instructional Strategies

Some assessment of the new teacher's range of teaching strategies
should be made. This can be done through self-assessment. Depend-

ing on where the teacher was trained and her degree of past experience, the level of competence in different teaching strategies will
vary significantly from teacher to teacher. Most districts now offer
some variation of in-service in the direct instruction model. If this
model has become incorporated into the district, if a common vocab-
ulary exists which is used to discuss instruction, and if it is used in
the observation/evaluation of teachers, the anticipatory teacher
must be oriented to the model. *Models of Teaching* (Joyce and Weil,
1972) is a classic compendium of instructional strategies and could
serve as the basis for additional in-service sessions not only for anticipatory teachers, but also for the whole staff.

Student Needs

The anticipatory teacher should understand the characteristics of
the general student population. Facts regarding socioeconomic class,
general achievement, family composition, ethnic background, and
social behavior patterns would be helpful. Percentages of students
attending higher educational institutions, literacy rate of parents,
education level of parents, and longevity in the district would also be
beneficial in providing the anticipatory teacher with a better
understanding of the students. Information about students with special problems should be made available, along with district contact
persons who could provide the new teacher with additional information.

Assessment/Evaluation

Several sessions may be required to explain the district's assess-
ment/evaluation program. New teachers need an orientation to the
district's use of standardized achievement tests, criterion referenced
tests, state mandated tests, year-end tests, report cards, grading
practices, and parent conferences. Lessons in how to use and interpret data in the student's permanent record are also advised.

Managerial Needs

Managerial needs for the anticipatory teacher include those
related to scheduling, facilities, classroom management, and discipline. Teachers need to understand how students are assigned to

classes, what pull-out programs may impact on the instructional time available, what planning time is scheduled, when teachers meet to confer about an individual student, what support services are available, what interruptions may be expected during the day or the year, and any other information which would help the teacher plan the school year.

Facilities

Anticipatory teachers would benefit from a tour of the whole district and the community served. The extent of the tour would be determined by the size of the district and the available time. If possible, elementary school teachers should have an opportunity to walk through the high school and middle school facilities, because it is important for new teachers to see how instruction at their level fits into instruction at another level. Anything that would help the new teachers gain a better understanding of the students they serve and the community in which they work would be valuable.

Classroom Management/Discipline

Special attention should be given to classroom management and discipline. If the board of education has adopted policies that address this area, they should be shared with new teachers. Building-level discipline codes in place at all levels in the system should also be among the materials given to the anticipatory teacher.

Of even greater significance are workshops in the area of classroom management, because this area typically causes the new teacher the most difficulty. In an effort to be accepted and liked by students, the new teacher frequently fails to set high levels of expectation for acceptable student behavior. Rules and standards are developed after repeated infractions by students rather than before disruptive behavior occurs, and new teachers need to understand the importance of establishing these standards on the very first day of class. Setting high expectations alone will not prevent students from testing the rules. The anticipatory teacher would benefit greatly from training sessions that explain techniques for handling off-task behavior. Most districts have a number of books, articles, and audiovisual materials that address this topic. A bibliography of these materials could be assembled and provided to the new teachers. Teachers in the system who have exemplary classroom management techniques could be identified and listed as possible contact/resource persons for the new staff. The new staff should be informed in the orientation sessions that assistance is available to any new teacher experiencing difficulty in this crucial area. Classroom management problems are common for new teachers and are not to be perceived as a sign of failure. Failure would be for the new teacher not to seek help.

Informational Needs

The furthest thing from the anticipatory teacher's mind is the district's policy manual. Most new teachers don't have the foggiest idea about what policy development is, much less understand the tenuous relationship between the Board's function as a policy development body and the administration's function of carrying out the policy of the district. New teachers should be supplied with information about the policies, procedures, routines, and mores of the district.

Policy

Board policies that have a direct bearing on teacher behavior should be made available to new teachers. For example, every new teacher is interested in the benefit package offered by a district, as well as her negotiated contract. New teachers are rarely interested in the district's policy manual. If the policy manual is up to date and in compliance with state law, codes, and regulations, part of it should be required reading for new teachers. Topics like confidentiality of student information, teacher and student evaluation procedures, child abuse, AIDS, and student discipline are addressed in school policy manuals and have a direct bearing on what is acceptable behavior for the new teacher.

A review of the district's policy manual is also an effective way to make teachers aware of the school organizational structure and to review the district's chain of command. Teachers frequently become irate when Board members are approached directly by citizens about a problem which was never discussed with the teacher. Administrators feel the same way about teachers who go directly to board members and bypass the internal chain of command.

Procedures

Most districts have a procedures manual which accompanies the policy manual and provides the pragmatics for carrying out the district's policies. The procedures manual is usually available in the principal's office. New teachers should know where the manual is located and what it addresses. Procedures that are unique to a building ought to be included in the building's student-faculty handbook. This document should be made available to every teacher working in the building. It is important to keep this document current and up-to-date. If a building committee to review and update the building handbook exists, it is a good idea to include an anticipatory teacher on the committee to ensure that the manual addresses the needs and concerns of teachers at this career stage.

It would be impossible to address all of the policy and procedure issues which anticipatory teachers need to know in the initial orientation sessions. Therefore, it is important that a series of meetings be held in the course of the first two years of service in the district. As the teacher becomes familiar with the district, the information becomes more and more relevant. Unless the administration plans to provide this information formally, teachers will attempt to get it when they face a crisis. Too often, the solutions to a problem are sought in the teachers' room, but unfortunately, the solutions offered by other teachers are not always based on complete knowledge of district policy or procedure. Sometimes the solutions offered in the teachers' room are ones which transfer ownership of a problem from the teacher to the district administration.

Routines

Most school routines are unwritten and the new teacher learns them by modeling other teachers. Routines for getting students into the classroom, taking attendance, reporting illness, ordering chalk, requesting parent conferences, and dismissing students are just a few. These routines can best be taught by forming a mentor relationship between a new teacher and an expert/master teacher (Lowney, 1986). Since this relationship is not a line or staff relationship, the new teacher tends to use the mentor as a confidant, a source of personal support and guidance apart from the system's formal administrative structure. When this relationship is working well, the mentor teacher may be able to provide peer coaching, guide the new teacher to sources of professional information which will enable her to expand her talents, and provide the teacher with the emotional support necessary to overcome difficult times and continue to work toward becoming an expert/master teacher.

Mores

The mores of every school system are different. What is acceptable in one system may be totally unacceptable in another system. Mores are often learned by listening to sentences that begin with "That's not the . . . way," or "The way we do it here is . . . ." Initial acceptance of a new teacher depends on whether she is perceived as fitting in to the environment, as having values and beliefs that are similar to those of the other teachers. The problem of mores is more acute when new staff members are younger than the majority of the rest of the staff. If the gestalt created by a mature faculty with a mean age of fifty typifies a sense of withdrawal, the new anticipatory teacher will experience more difficulty accepting the mores of the faculty than if the environment were typified by a mature staff of expert/master teachers where renewal is an expectation.

Evaluative Needs

After anticipatory teachers have been in the system for several months and have experienced at least one formal observation, the entire procedure for evaluation and continuation of employment becomes increasingly important. Most school systems are required by law to notify non-tenured staff regarding continuation of contract by the end of April. School boards typically take this action in March or April. However, if the state code requires two or three observations prior to making the decision, by January a tentative decision is being formulated. The evaluation procedure and the instruments used for the process should be reviewed with anticipatory teachers early in the fall of their first year of employment.

Evaluation procedures which are of interest to the anticipatory teacher are not confined to the anticipatory teacher's evaluation. New teachers are equally interested in how supervisors, administrators, and programs are evaluated, what input they have in the evaluation of their superiors and how program evaluation affects their personal performance. If student achievement data are included as part of the teacher's evaluation, how is that done? Are final scores alone used, or student growth scores? What other student achievement data are used, such as criterion reference tests, student opinion polls, letters of commendation, and parent testimony? Are the decisions based solely on academic student growth, or are considerations given to social development, human relations skills, and other, less quantitative areas of student growth?

In reality, within most school systems, the three areas of evaluation: teacher, administrator, and program, operate independently. If that is the case, the anticipatory teacher should know it, and if it isn't, she needs to know how the three interface.

An induction program which addresses these five critical needs: psycho-social, educational, managerial, informational, and evaluative would greatly enhance the chances of the anticipatory teacher to move from idealism and naiveté to the self-assured expert/master teacher in the short period of time before tenure is granted.

SUPERVISION OF ANTICIPATORY TEACHERS

Presently, the granting of tenure is time-driven rather than competency-driven. Usually, a teacher who has worked in the system for three years and has not been told otherwise, receives tenure. Gaining this status does not require action by the board of education, rather, action is required only if tenure is not being granted.

The assumption here is that all teachers have the appropriate training, personal qualities, and potential for being expert/master teachers. This fact is validated by the certification they hold. Following this assumption, a teacher who does not become an expert/master teacher would be the exception, rather than the rule. Using this line of reasoning, if the teacher does not become an expert/master teacher, it surely must be the fault of the system, the students, or the parents, and this is the logic employed by most teacher unions and courts. It is becoming increasingly difficult to dismiss even the non-tenured teacher.

Does this mean that the training received in our teacher preparation institutions is so superior that the newly certified teacher can easily demonstrate expert/master qualities in two to three years? Hardly so, according to recent studies of our higher education teacher training institutions, like the Holmes Report, the Carnegie Report, and others.

To grant tenure to a teacher who is not an expert/master teacher,

is to say to the students, the parents, the Board, and the public that
the goal of the system is to be average.

The reputation of a school district is determined by the reputation
of the people employed by the district. One would be hard pressed to
find a school system with a long-standing reputation of excellence,
populated with a majority of average teachers, average administrators, and an average Board.

Taking the position that the teacher must demonstrate that he/she
is in the expert/master teacher stage prior to receiving tenure places
a whole new level of importance on this career stage. Rather than
viewing these teachers as new to the system and still learning, this
career stage requires them to demonstrate their skills.

The system's expectations should be made clear to these teachers
when they are hired. By the time they begin their third year of
teaching, they should be able to demonstrate their competence.

During the first year of employment, the teacher and her immediate supervisor should develop a three-year plan to be approved by
the principal and placed in the teacher's personnel file. This plan
should detail the categories in which the teacher expects to demonstrate competency at the beginning of the third year, and list the
types of indicators which can be observed to verify these competencies.

Applied here, it would mean that non-tenured teachers working in
the system would identify their own competencies, write competency
statements, discuss these statements with the administrator to be
sure the statement reflects the intent of the desired competency,
demonstrate their competency behaviorally, and have the administrator verify their achievement of the competency.

The areas in which the anticipatory teacher could demonstrate
competency should be mutually agreed upon by the teacher and the
administrator. A list of possible areas includes:

- lesson development
- assessing student needs
- evaluating the learner
- parent and community relations
- knowledge of subject
- motivation of students
- development of learning climate
- understanding child development and growth
- involvement in the total school community

—classroom management
—use of instructional materials
—evidence of continued professional growth

Competency Development

The process has two basic steps, clarification and verification. After the competency categories are identified, the non-tenured teacher begins the daily routine of teaching, and within a short period of time, she will be able to demonstrate competency in a number of the specified areas. When the teacher believes that she is ready to verify a skill at the expert/master teacher level, she will write the statement down. An example of a statement which could be included in the category "lesson development" follows: "Consistently develops lessons which include the critical elements of direct instruction." After the statement is written, the teacher should meet with the supervisor, department chairperson, or principal to have the statement clarified.

Clarification simply means ascertaining that the statement says what the teacher wants it to say, that the words are precise and clear, and that the statement is succinct and represents a competency indicative of an expert/master teacher. If the statement meets all of these criteria, the administrator initials the statement.

While there is no particular form for these statements, using file cards is an effective way of organizing them. Each statement of competency would be written on a single file card. The cards could then be filed under the appropriate categories as they are developed. The decision to accept a competency as indicative of skills at the expert/master stage would be mutually agreed upon by the teacher and the administrator.

Competency Verification

After the statement is clarified, the teacher decides what evidence will be used for verification. In the example given above, the verification may be based on a review of lesson plans over a period of two or three months. At the time of verification, the administrator reviews the evidence and, if it is satisfactory, signs off on the competency. Once verification has been given, the administrator may reduce the requirements for documenting the competency. Lesson plan development may not need to be as formalized as it was before the demonstration of competency.

Competency clarification and verification would be incorporated into the clinical supervisory process used with anticipatory teachers. The pre-conference would be a time for a general review of the progress being made. It would also be a time for clarification, for identifying areas still to be developed, and for reviewing evidence for verification. If the teacher possesses the competency at the expert/master teacher stage, it should be clearly visible on a consistent basis.

The classroom observation would include behavioral verification of the competency, which the administrator can accomplish by simply examining the teacher's behavior in front of her class.

The post-conference would provide an opportunity for the administrator to sign off on the verified competencies and a time to discuss additional competencies to be achieved.

The post-conference is also the appropriate time for the teacher to provide feedback to the administrator regarding the teacher's development and integration into the system (Sullivan, 1980).

CURRICULUM MONITORING OF ANTICIPATORY TEACHERS

Each new anticipatory teacher should be supplied with a copy of the district's curriculum for the content area and grade level being taught. It is assumed here that the written curriculum has been aligned with the tested curriculum. It is further assumed that the written curriculum is the appropriate and desired one for the subject and the grade level. If it isn't, the district has no right to hold the teacher responsible for the student's achievements. It is the teacher's responsibility to deliver the appropriate curriculum. It is not the responsibility of the anticipatory teacher to align the written and tested curricula. Assuring quality control in curriculum management is the responsibility of the administration.

When the anticipatory teacher receives a copy of the written curriculum, she should be confident that it states the desired expectations for students, and that the instructional materials available to the teacher are appropriate for the delivery of the curriculum.

After the teacher becomes familiar with the written curriculum for the year, the curriculum K–12 for the subject level should be reviewed so that the teacher can clearly see how the instruction for his/her assignment fits into the total program. By reviewing the written curriculum, the teacher should also be able to assess the skill level of students entering his/her classroom.

While all students may not have achieved all of the competencies, objectives, and proficiencies stated in the guide from the previous year, the average student should have.

Shortly after the year begins, the teacher should be able to develop a curriculum delivery chart that details the sequencing of units and the amount of time to be spent on each unit. This chart may differ from the one in the curriculum guide because it will be based on the teacher's assessment of the actual skill level of the students in the class. The chart should be completed by the end of September.

The chart should also include the dates of the district's formal testing program. This chart reminds the teacher to plan to deliver instruction in areas that are to be assessed on the standardized tests before the tests are given.

This is also an appropriate time for the teacher to review with the supervisor the results of previous tests for each of the students in the class. Most testing companies can supply item analysis data for each student which include an assessment of the student's potential compared with the student's actual achievement.

In making decisions about the sequence of instruction, anticipatory teachers should use standardized student data as one of the components to be reviewed; however, they should not rely solely on these data.

Curriculum guides are often organized in such a way that they detail the sequence of the presentation of knowledge in close parallel to the chapters in the text. The guide will often have a separate listing of the skills and concepts the students are expected to master. However, it will be necessary for the anticipatory teacher to provide the integration that the guide does not cover.

This can be accomplished by the teacher identifying the units of study and listing the knowledge, skills, and concepts which will be stressed in each one. If there are skills and concepts that will be integrated into the instruction for the entire year, they should be so stated. To leave the integration to chance, is to lose the opportunity to maximize the effective and efficient use of instructional time.

Once the curriculum delivery chart has been completed and the units of instruction detailed, the teacher can begin to focus on the development of detailed lesson plans to achieve her objectives. Anticipatory teachers should continue to develop formalized lesson plans until they have clarified and verified their competency in this area.

REWARDING THE ANTICIPATORY TEACHER

Teachers at all career stages should feel that they are rewarded by the system. Teaching is a difficult, demanding occupation. Without sufficient reward, teachers will seek employment in other, more lucrative professions. Teaching has never been viewed as a financially rewarding profession. Only within the past few years has attention to entry-level teacher salaries been the concern of state legislatures. When the state of New Jersey passed legislation which placed the teacher minimum salary at $18,500, it created headlines across the United States.

The reward structure for the anticipatory teacher should not only make that teacher aware of the progress he/she is making toward becoming an expert/master teacher, but also link him/her to the national educational network. One way to accomplish this link is for the district to fund membership in a regional educational association for the anticipatory teacher. This membership will permit the teacher to meet other professional educators from various districts, and it allows him to develop contacts with educators who are interested in the same subjects as the anticipatory teacher. Teachers who are members of local professional organizations are more likely to be in the expert/master teacher stage than in the withdrawal stage. These organizations attempt to remain current in the field and to be on the cutting edge of the latest research, current thinking, newest materials, and innovative practices. Quite often membership brings with it a subscription to an educators journal. By being involved in this type of organization, the anticipatory teacher broadens his support base, such that when he faces a difficult problem, he is much more likely to call on someone he knows from the organization than to seek the help of a district administrator. The other advantage of linking the anticipatory teacher to the national educational network is that his knowledge about what is appropriate for the field immediately expands beyond the limits of the district that employs him. Without this linkage, the anticipatory teacher is limited to the level of knowledge of those teachers with whom he comes into contact. Sometimes this cadre is restricted to the teachers in the teacher's room who may or may not represent the best in current knowledge in the anticipatory teacher's area of instruction.

Questionnaires can be used periodically to assure that the administration is meeting the teacher's anticipatory needs. An example of one such questionnaire is included for your review. Results from the questionnaire could be useful in modifying district practices to be sure that these teachers feel they are involved in the district's decision-making process and to ensure that these teachers have the appropriate resources, feel supported by the district's administrators and feel adequately informed about district decisions.

Teacher Questionnaire—Anticipatory Stage

Most of you have been in your positions with this school system for less than six months. As you know, we view all non-tenured staff as being in the anticipatory stage of their career. This questionnaire was developed in an effort to help us better meet your needs. Responses will be anonymous and will be used collectively by central administration to identify patterns and trends of new teachers. There will be no attempt to identify individual responses.

In a recent study, "The Learning Workplace: The Conditions and Resources of Teaching," Samuel B. Bacharach, professor of organizational behavior at Cornell University, reported on a national survey of 1800 teachers. From this study, he concluded that teachers perceive a lack of:

—resources
—involvement in decision making
—frequency of communication with building administration
—supportive leadership from building administration

In an effort to assess your feelings regarding these areas and others, please respond to the following questions. Place your response in the envelope provided, seal it, and send it to the office of the superintendent.

1. Do you feel you have adequate, appropriate materials and supplies to carry out your teaching responsibilities? If not, how are they deficient?
2. As a new teacher in the system, were you involved in the budget development process this year? How? Were the materials and supplies you recommended purchased?
3. When you need audiovisual equipment to support instruction, is it available to you? Is it in good working order?
4. Have you had an opportunity to work directly with the media specialist in your building or request support from the media specialist? Are there ways we can improve the communication

between the media specialist and the classroom teacher? If so, please suggest them.

5. Has your opinion been solicited regarding the improvement of the educational program at the department, building, or district level? Address each level in responding.

6. Have you offered unsolicited suggestions for improvement of the educational program at the department, building, or district level? What happened to those suggestions?

7. Do you feel you are a contributing member of the professional staff and that your suggestions are heard and given as much consideration as the suggestions of more senior staff members? Why do you think this is so?

8. On approximately how many occasions have you had an opportunity to communicate with your department supervisor, if there is one, building administration, or central administration? Again, please address each level separately. How could the communication at each of these levels be improved?

9. Do you have a sense of where this district is headed? Is there a feeling that the leadership of the district is attempting to give it direction, or do you sense that the district is in a maintenance mode?

10. When you began the year, you were filled with excitement about being part of this district. How do you feel about the system now? Have your feelings changed, and if so, why?

11. Do you feel you receive supportive leadership from the administrators in the district? Why do you feel the way you do? What can we do to improve our skills in this area?

12. Please use this space to make any other comments you would like. Remember, the purpose of this questionnaire is to help us to more adequately meet your needs. Your comments and suggestions will enable us to do that. Thank you.

SUMMARY

Improving the quality of instruction in America's classrooms may depend mostly on the activities associated with the orientation and indoctrination of the anticipatory teacher. As present teachers retire and districts replace them, there will be an opportunity to upgrade the critical induction phase to increase the number of teachers moving from the anticipatory to the expert/master teacher stage during the two to three years prior to the granting of tenure.

Suggestions were made in this chapter to greatly improve the in-service training of these new teachers. It was noted that many states now require a formalized teacher induction process. This process should include extended teacher in-service, clinical supervision, close monitoring of curriculum, mentorships, and high pay for attaining higher standards.

Once on staff, these teachers tend to feel greater satisfaction from their jobs when they are involved in the decision-making process, given recognition for their accomplishments, and provided with a high degree of autonomy regarding the processes used to implement the curriculum (Brodinsky, 1984).

By establishing a competency clarification/verification process to document the anticipatory teacher's growth, the hard work expended is rewarded and recognized, growth efforts are directed, and areas for improvement become clear.

Facilitating membership in regional associations and keeping current in the literature of the field enable the anticipatory teacher to gain greater feelings of professionalism.

All this activity is directed toward supporting the teacher through this period of indoctrination and ascent to the coveted career stage of expert/master teacher.

INQUIRY

Questions and Answers About Chapter Three

Question #1: *Are all anticipatory teachers as exhilarating as you describe them here? Does the word anticipatory relate to a competency level or an attitude?*

Answer: Both! Anticipatory relates to attitude in that generally people who apply for new jobs want them and they are excited about getting them. It also relates to attitude in terms of how much experience the newly hired teacher may have as a practicing professional. If the teacher is newly certified, the chances are that he/she will more closely resemble the idealistic description presented in this chapter. If the newly hired teacher has been an expert/master teacher in another district, the level of idealism will not be as great. This is inversely true regarding the level of competency. If the anticipatory teacher is newly certified, the level of competency is not very great. However, if the anticipatory teacher had been an expert/master teacher in another district, the level of competency should be great. No matter what the prior experience level of the newly hired teacher, he/she enters the new work environment as an anticipatory teacher.

Question #2: *What appear to be the most common areas of teacher problems in the "anticipatory" stage and how have you dealt with them?*

Answer: Problems related to classroom management tend to be the most common among newly certified anticipatory teachers. These problems are generally solved by closely supervising the anticipatory teacher, allowing her an opportunity to observe teachers with good classroom management practices, and teaching her how to develop a lesson with tight structure, smooth transitions, and good pacing. This lesson should motivate and instruct the students at their own level of ability. The other common problem for anticipatory teachers is to find a way to continue their professional growth. Sometimes they believe that they have learned all they need to learn in order to be expert/master teachers; they do not realize that expert/master teachers are continually learning and improving their training. Encouraging them to continue to read professional journals, to take in-service courses, and to pursue advanced degrees, all help to expand their level of knowledge and skill.

Question #3: *Do all teachers go through the anticipatory stage? Isn't it possible for some to be very close to the expert/master stage at the outset?*

Answer: Yes, as stated earlier, all newly hired teachers enter at the anticipatory stage. The length of time spent at that stage depends on the level of competency they possess when they arrive. It would be highly unlikely for even the most skilled professional to reach the expert/master teacher stage until the second half of the first year. For others, the anticipatory stage could be extended beyond the non-tenured period. In most cases the district is unwilling to take a chance by extending tenure to a teacher who is still operating at the anticipatory stage after three years.

Question #4: *The career stages model assumes that nearly every teacher is, at some time, in the anticipatory stage. Is there any stage that is in-between, i.e., post collegiate but pre-anticipatory? If so, what is it and what do you do about it?*

Answer: This model does not address an in-between stage. The question seems to suggest that this may be someone who graduates with an educational degree but is not sure she wants to teach, or someone who has not been able to find a job in the field. Both of these situations fall outside this model.

Question #5: *How long does the anticipatory stage accurately describe the internal career orientation of most teachers? What seem to be the factors that separate teachers with respect to how long they remain at this stage?*

Answer: The word anticipatory describes the teacher who is still becoming familiar with the work environment and who is not displaying a skill level that is acknowledged as being highly effective in facilitating student learning. The amount of prior experience and the skill level achieved during this experience are the two factors that most commonly differentiate the length of time teachers spend in the anticipatory stage.

REFERENCES

BELASCO, J. and J. Alutto. "Decisional Participation and Teacher Satisfaction," *Educational Administration Quarterly*, Volume VIII, #31, pp. 44–58 (1972).

BRODINSKY, B. "Teacher Morale; What Builds It; What Kills It." *Instructor*, p. 36 (April 1984).

JOYCE, B. and M. Weil. *Models of Teaching*. New Jersey:Prentice-IIall (1972).

LEATHERMAN. "Reforms in Education of School Teachers Facing Tough New Challenges," *Chronicle of Higher Education*, 34, p. 1, A30–36 (April 20, 1988).

LOWNEY, R. G. *Mentor Teachers: The California Model*. Bloomington, Indiana:The Phi Delta Kappa Educational Foundation (1986).

SULLIVAN, C. G. *Clinical Supervision*. Association for Supervision and Curriculum Development (1980).

Current Research 1986 Teacher Induction. Pennsylvania Association for Supervision and Curriculum Development.

The expert/master teacher.

The Expert/Master Teacher Stage

BEYOND IRREDUCIBILITY

THE class of the teaching cadre is the expert/master teacher. They are the ones who are acknowledged by their peers, by the administration, and by the students and parents to be *the best*. Their characteristics, even their quirks, are part of the definition of the superb professional. No matter how precise the description of this professional, there is always something absolutely irreducible about them. At some point, they simply can't be defined any more specifically than the language allows, or all meaning is lost about the whole.

For example, consider the description of one of the greatest American courtroom lawyers:

> (his) . . . manner was easygoing and relaxed, almost casual. Behind the facade of laziness operated a first-class mind always working at top speed and efficiency; on his feet he was a master of phrase-making. Afterward, it was hard to remember his precise gestures and actions in the courtroom, because one listened carefully to what he said and observed less what he did. He kept his thumbs in his colorful galluses most of the time and his gestures, rather than being motions of his arms and hands, were made with his head and shoulders, he would thrust his face toward the court. It was a central characteristic . . . that he engaged his listeners' minds, not their eyes (Scopes, 1967, p. 112).

The lawyer was none other than Clarence Darrow, the relentless cross-examiner whose passionate courtroom inquiries have been made the subject of broadway plays and movies. Clarence Darrow had been a teacher in Ohio for three years, and in all probability he had not been an expert/master teacher. He confessed in his autobiography (1932, p. 28) that over three years, he taught approximately fifty students, ranging in ages from seven years to one or two years beyond his own age, and "I am not sure how much I taught the pupils, but I am certain that they taught me. I tried to make (them) happy even if I could not make them wise."

From what we know about expert/master teachers, Darrow was on the right track. His comments about his own primary education make it clear that he found school largely dull and disconnected from the world. He focused on his pupils.

Few accounts of Darrow's actions in court would get more specific and delve into what made him so spectacularly effective as a courtroom lawyer than the record supplied by defendant Scopes. There are virtually no descriptions of him as a classroom teacher.

We have apparently reached the level of irreducibility of Clarence Darrow as a teacher and a lawyer. Despite the passage of time, we don't get much closer to precision than we've just encountered. Undoubtedly, many readers will have the urge to say "yes, yes, I know all that, but what is it that makes the expert/master teacher?" However, we can only offer suggestions, hints, descriptions, and narrative, because if we knew the answer, we might also know more about the minds of Shakespeare, Beethoven, or Einstein. Rather than simply ending the discussion, let us proceed as best we can.

A FACILITATOR OF HUMAN DEVELOPMENT

The expert/master teacher is a facilitator of human development above all else. Gazda (1973, p. 8) defines this person as "one who helps unfold the human potential of a student through guiding and strengthening him."

With the help of the expert/master teacher the student becomes an adult who "understands, respects and acts upon his own thoughts, feelings and experiences . . .", in addition to "understanding, respecting and acting in response to the thoughts, feelings, and experiences of others."

CHARACTERISTICS OF THE EXPERT/MASTER TEACHER

Expert/master teachers come in all ages, sizes, and shapes. They are of all races and both genders. The expert/master teacher exemplifies the helping role of the perceiver created by Carkhuff (1969, 1971, and 1972) with its eight characteristics:

Empathy	Depth/understanding
Respect	Belief in
Warmth	Caring/love
Concreteness	Ability to be specific
Genuineness	Honesty/realness
Self-disclosure	Ability to convey appropriately "I've been there too."
Confrontation	Pointing to our discrepancies
Immediacy	Telling it like it is between helper and helpee

The first three characteristics are important in building rapport with the student. In this phase the teacher earns the right to be the teacher, a right earned through expressions of tenderness, which carries with it the teacher's ability to take risks with the learner and to do what is necessary to accomplish the goals of learning. Tenderness is not to be confused with permissiveness. Tenderness may mean strict discipline, adherence to classroom routines, pressing the student to the limit of his/her abilities.

The last three characteristics: self-disclosure, confrontation, and immediacy refer to the time when the teacher displays self-confidence and in depth knowledge of his/her field. The teacher uses the first three characteristics when she is getting to know the class. This phase is referred to as the helpee-exploration phase. The next three characteristics describe the understanding phase, which occurs when the teacher is "putting oneself in the shoes of another" and "seeing through the eyes of another." The last phase is the action phase. The teacher knows the class, its potential, its individual members, the expectations it can achieve, and the success it can enjoy.

While the Carkhuff model speaks eloquently to the process the expert/master teacher uses, school effectiveness research has identified numerous specific characteristics of the teacher at this career stage (AASA, 1986, p. 4). Expert/master teachers tend to:

—be good managers
—use systematic instruction techniques
—have high expectations of their students and themselves
—believe in their own efficacy

—vary teaching strategies
—handle discipline through presentation
—be warm and caring
—be democratic in their approach
—be task-oriented
—be concerned with perceptual meanings rather than
  facts and events
—be comfortable in interacting with students
—have a strong grasp of the subject matter
—be readily accessible to students outside of class
—tailor their teaching to student needs
—be highly flexible, enthusiastic, and imaginative

Each of us can probably name a few expert/master teachers. Those I was fortunate enough to have known through the years had many of the same characteristics:

Mrs. Green was my junior high school home economics teacher, and one of her characteristics I remember most was her accepting attitude toward me. I wasn't the brightest or the best student in the class, but I knew I was "okay" in Mrs. Green's book and that was really all that mattered. Because of her accepting attitude, I really did try my best to do well in her class. I knew Mrs. Green was interested in me as a person and my relationship with her continued for twenty years until her death. Mrs. Green was an expert/master teacher from my point of view.

Mr. Thompson was known as the strictest teacher in high school; he rarely smiled and set high standards for his students. We had homework every night and the tests were "killers." But Mr. Thompson had a way of making chemistry come alive. His lectures were like listening to fairy tales, only the characters were elements and compounds. Because of his inspiration, I entered pharmacy school. Mr. Thompson also was an expert/master teacher.

Pat Blackburn is a physical education teacher, and nothing bothers her more than to hear parents, students, or other teachers bad-mouth physical education teachers. Pat believes in bell-to-bell instruction and in pushing her students to the limit. She runs a no-nonsense class that focuses on developing sound physical fitness skills for students. Students listen attentively and watch as Pat demonstrates a new skill to be learned. Because Pat is also a coach, she is able to develop personal relationships with many of her students. They trust her and confide in her. She loves teaching and consistently rejects attempts to interest her in an administrative position.

Marcia Stevens is the Pied Piper of Wilson Elementary. Being a large woman, there is always room on her lap for at least three children. Every child is a winner in Marcia's class. Students arrive early to carry her things to her room, and there are always two or three boys who find an excuse to stay after school to help her. When class is in session, her room is as active as a beehive. It could be described as organized chaos. Marcia keeps a record of her former students' achievements. Among their ranks are senators, doctors, scientists, and community leaders, and they frequently name her in public presentations when they are questioned about significant teachers in their lives.

This book could be filled with vignettes of expert/master teachers. My purpose for including the brief sketches that appear here is to point out the diversity of these special educators. Expert/master teachers are easy to recognize, because there is an unmistakable synergy in their classrooms. Is it art or is it science? I believe it is a combination of the two.

Much knowledge on effective teaching has been accumulated and should be taught in teacher training institutions, but the art of teaching, that which originates from experience combined with the teacher's personality, cannot be taught.

Little more than 200 years ago, less than twenty percent of the nation's children were attending school, because parents had to pay for the privilege. By the late 1800s, however, the nation had established free public education, and today, nearly forty million students in the United States receive their education from some 2.7 million educators (Parsons, 1985, p. 15).

Not all of these teachers are at the anticipatory stage, the expert/master teacher stage, or in renewal. We owe it to the children we serve to do everything in our power to increase the number of teachers at the expert/master stage and decrease the number of those in withdrawal.

The critical mix of teachers at the various stages in a building or a district sets the tone for the school or district. In the introduction to chapter one of Parson's book, Harold Howe II, senior lecturer at the Harvard Graduate School of Education, describes the ethos of a school as ". . . its capacity to promote association among children and adults in ways to bring out the best in both and to make the school a place where respect, integrity, and affection set the tone for human relationship" (p. 16). Howe describes a school populated by a large percentage of teachers at the expert/master teacher level or ones seeking that level through renewal. If we are going to attempt to maintain our expert/master teachers at this stage, we need to know and satisfy their needs.

IN-SERVICE FOR THE EXPERT/MASTER TEACHER

The expert/master teacher thrives on all kinds of in-service. These are the teachers who usually provide the highest ratings for the speakers on in-service days. While these large group sessions are nice times to get the entire faculty together, their greatest benefit is not the growth of staff expertise. Rather they serve as an opportunity for staff to have a break from the daily routine of their classroom responsibilities, the chance for teachers to see other teachers in the district, and almost always as a topic for teacher room discussion for a few days after the session. Then, it's business as usual.

Teacher in-service that is effective in changing the behavior patterns of teachers, as described by Joyce (1983, p. 83–86) includes five critical steps:

—presentation of theory
—modeling or demonstration
—practice under simulated conditions
—structured feedback
—coaching for application

These five steps are necessary for learning a new skill no matter what career stage the teacher is in. The first step requires learning about some new thing, which can be accomplished through reading and attending workshops, lectures, or even large group staff in-service sessions. This step is similar to Bloom's (1965) lowest level of learning, developing a knowledge base. The problem with many district in-service programs is that the knowledge component is seen as the beginning and the end of the in-service. The other mistake is assuming that the entire faculty is interested in the same growth area.

The second step in Joyce's model requires the new skill to be modeled or demonstrated. This means that the teacher attempting to learn the new skill has an opportunity to see it in action. If the district is fortunate enough to have a resident expert in the skill, he can provide demonstration lessons for the staff. If not, the demonstration may be on film. Perhaps a teacher in a nearby district has acquired the skill and would agree to have her class video taped. In one district I know of, the entire staff was receiving in-service on the direct instruction model. A consultant had been hired to provide the knowledge base. Teachers met in small groups of twenty-five with the teacher trainer for two days of intensive in-service. On the afternoon of the second day, one of the teachers participating in the in-service presented a video tape which demonstrated some of the skills that had been discussed. In this particular district, with approximately 235 professional staff persons, it took nine weeks to in-service the entire staff. Nine different teachers prepared video tapes to demonstrate selected skills from the lectures. The district had nine potential coaches for helping other teachers take the in-service from the knowledge step to the application step.

The third step involves practice under simulated conditions. One way to achieve this is to offer after-school courses for credit whose curriculum consists of practice under simulated conditions. The district mentioned above intends to provide such an in-service course. Teachers interested in perfecting their skills in the direct instruction model will be encouraged to take the course for credit and movement on the salary schedule. Although many expert/master teachers are already at the top of the salary guide and their continued growth does not result in any additional compensation through the union contract, they still comprise a large percentage of those attending the in-service courses.

This follow-up course will not only be used by teachers who voluntarily want to learn the new skills, but will also be highly recommended to those teachers at both the anticipatory and the withdrawal stage who would benefit from the experience.

If the skill being developed is one exhibited by a small group of teachers, or only one teacher, then alternate ways of providing the practice under simulated conditions have to be found. Two teachers could team up together, one who has the skill and one who does not. This arrangement could offer opportunities for demonstration and practice. In addition, it could illustrate the fourth step which is structured feedback.

Structured feedback occurs when the teacher who is trying the skill is observed by someone who understands the skill well enough to break it down into its discrete parts and knows how to correct any deficiencies. Structured feedback should be provided by an expert. Perhaps a teacher who is proficient in the skill could be given some release time to assist other teachers. If the number of teachers who want to acquire the skill is sufficiently large, the district may consider hiring a coach for the program, one whose primary responsibility is to help teachers make the skills operational.

The video camera can also be used to provide the teacher with structured feedback. The time seems to have passed when video cameras were certain to heighten the anxiety level of both students and teachers in classrooms. Now it is almost impossible to keep them out of the classroom. The number of video cameras being purchased by parents, intent on providing a pictorial account of their childrens' school years, is dramatically increasing, as the prices of video cameras decline. Perhaps this is an opportunity educators can capitalize upon.

Coaching for application is the final necessary step in the acquisition of a new skill. At this time the skill becomes integrated into the repertoire of the teacher, who can then modify it, embellish it, or expand it. It is at this level that the teacher needs a cheerleader; someone to help sustain the momentum when it doesn't work. A full-time coach is probably not realistic for most districts, but a recognized expert could be hired to periodically visit teachers interested in feedback, and provide them with informal suggestions for effectively implementing the skill. Ideally, the department chairperson, supervisor, or building principal would assume the role. This means that their level of expertise is such that they could serve in this role and are perceived by the rest of the staff as having the skills at the expert/master level. If this isn't the case, perhaps in-service activities should be considered for the administrators.

In any in-service effort, it is important to remember that no way of teaching is appropriate for all students. Teaching is a series of decisions about a multitude of things and adding to the skill base of the faculty is a way of increasing the probability that the match between the teacher's skills and the student's learning needs is met.

Growth opportunities for the expert/master teacher generally lie outside the district. These teachers are regarded as the in-house experts for many staff development activities in the district. Their own needs to grow, and they are strong needs, are met by continually expanding their skill and knowledge base. It is important that each expert/master teacher be permitted to seek out growth experiences. When the administrator receives notices announcing workshops, conferences, or meetings, he should examine them with the idea that they may be in-service opportunities for an expert/master teacher.

At the end of each month, the building administrator should review the staff in the building, and reflect upon the in-service opportunities that have been offered. The district may want to publish a periodic staff renewal bulletin listing and describing the activities in which staff has engaged. Who knows, another teacher in the district may have the same interests. This bulletin could also serve as an in-service item for the rest of the staff, letting them know what kind of activities are going on. It would also send a clear message to the staff that this is a district interested in supporting teacher growth, and this is how it is being done. As the expert/master teacher moves through Joyce's five steps, administrators must be creative in supplying the resources necessary to support his/her growth. Expert/master teachers are used to providing their own renewal and growth, which is probably how they arrived at the expert/master teacher stage. This model asks administrators to be more cognizant of the means and methods used by expert/master teachers to attain that career stage, and then apply those practices that help them maintain the stage.

SUPERVISION OF THE EXPERT/MASTER TEACHER

When I began my teaching career, I lived in the state of Pennsylvania. Teacher observation, supervision, and evaluation were all combined into one simple state required document to which we referred as Deb 333. It consisted of a brief checklist of skills, and required the building administrator to indicate whether the teacher was satisfactory or unsatisfactory. It was a joke!

The implication for me was that the expectations for teachers in the state of Pennsylvania were simply that they perform at a satisfactory level. Perhaps educators find themselves viewed with skepticism by the private business sector, many parents, most politicians, and large numbers of students, because they sometimes lower their expectations to meet the state's floor objective.

From my perspective, the methods and instruments used to observe, supervise, and evaluate teachers set the expectation level for all teachers' performance. Teachers are very explicit about the observation, supervision, and evaluation of student performance. The art of student evaluation has been perfected by some teachers who can easily distinguish differences in student performance, such as between an "A" or an "A −" or between a "B −" and a "C +". Students don't seem to have any difficulty accepting the teacher's ability to make these judgments and only occasionally question the validity of the grade given. Teachers are expected to be proficient in observing, supervising, and evaluating students with wide differences in ability, learning styles, and varying socio-economic levels.

On the other hand, with respect to the observation, supervision, and evaluation of teachers, administrators are often made to appear as simpletons. I urge administrators to be just as good at evaluating teachers as teachers are at evaluating students. Expert/master teachers observe, supervise, and evaluate student performance with skill and accuracy. Expert/master administrators can and should evaluate teachers with the same skill. Rating the teacher as satisfactory or unsatisfactory is not acceptable.

The purpose of evaluating students is to provide them with feedback on their performance, and this should be the same for teachers. Supervision should not be viewed as an end, but as a means to an end. At the expert/master teacher level, supervision should facilitate the growth and development of the already exemplary skills of the teacher. For him, supervision includes providing himself with the coaching support he may need to continue growth activities.

Just as an "A" student will more than likely continue to be an "A" student, the evaluation of an expert/master teacher using the same methods year after year will produce the predicted superior rating. While it is nice to receive two or three such assessments, they can fail to provide the expert/master teacher with the feedback necessary to perfect a new skill.

If the teacher's contract specifies a certain type of teacher assessment procedure, by all means follow the procedure. But this should be considered simply the base for the expert/master teacher. The student aiming for a score of 800 on the math section of the SAT doesn't get excited about passing the minimum competence test for the state. Likewise, the expert/master teacher who knows just how good she is doesn't have the latest Deb 333 framed on the classroom wall. I believe that contracted observation, supervision, and evaluation practices should be treated like minimum competency testing. It provides a floor.

The supervisory model designed to support the maintenance of the expert/master teacher has to be individualized. If the teacher is attempting to become proficient with Hilda Taba's Inductive Model (1962), the observation procedures used to provide that teacher with appropriate feedback might be vastly different from the observation procedures used to provide feedback for the teacher wanting to perfect the use of advanced organizers in the Hunter Model (1982).

The supervisory model to be used with any teacher should be discussed with him and be mutually agreed upon before the observation begins. It is almost like designing the evaluation component for a unit of instruction. At the end of the instruction, students should be able to demonstrate certain proficiencies. It is not different for the growth experience of a teacher. At the end of a given year, the teacher should be able to demonstrate new levels of proficiency. If this is not happening, new learning is not taking place. The supervisory function should establish a mechanism to document that continued growth.

Certainly every administrator is not going to be proficient with every observation instrument. An average district of 2500 pupils and five buildings with principals, assistant principals, and supervisors, may have an administrative cadre of fifteen to twenty people. If each administrator sets a yearly goal of becoming proficient at one new observation instrument, within two or three years, administrators in the district would be able to use multiple observation instruments to give teachers feedback about their performance.

Teachers would be free to designate the person and the procedure to be used to provide feedback to them. The results of a Flanders would be much more meaningful to the teacher if her objective was to promote a better balance between teacher talk and student talk.

If teachers are interested in perfecting their skills at peer observation, why not train teachers to be observers as well? True, some states require that in order to evaluate a teacher, one must be certified as an administrator. However, this does not prevent teachers from giving other teachers informal feedback, even if these peer observation documents do not become a part of the teachers' personnel file, so what? A teacher's real growth doesn't come from the administrators' name on the papers in the personnel file; it comes from real teachers interacting with real administrators, students, and fellow teachers in the day-to-day instruction of the school program.

Supervision of the expert/master teacher should take whatever form necessary to support the teacher's growth and should not be limited to contractually agreed upon instruments and procedures.

CURRICULUM MONITORING OF THE
EXPERT/MASTER TEACHER

All teachers, no matter what the career stage, need to adhere to the district curriculum, and mechanisms should be in place to ensure that this is happening. Of course, all this is predicated on the assumption that the system's curriculum has been clearly defined, subject area by subject area, and grade level by grade level. Finally, it is based on the supposition that there is agreement between the objectives to be achieved, the ability level of the students, and the amount of instructional time allotted to reach the desired objectives. The layperson reading this paragraph may question why it would be necessary to write it. Only educators know how unrealistic these basic assumptions are for too many subject areas and grade levels.

Unless these assumptions are met, curriculum monitoring practices are difficult, if not impossible to develop or maintain.

The expert/master teacher, by whatever means, has been able to fulfill these assumptions. The definition of what the district curriculum is, may differ from expert/master teacher to expert/master teacher, because if it is not specified clearly by the district, the expert/master teacher specifies it for himself. In making the decisions regarding the content of the curriculum for the year, the teacher takes into consideration the match between district objectives and student ability level. The expert/master teacher has also answered the question about instructional time. The amount of instructional time available is the driving force behind the answers to the first two questions. The expert/master teacher always leaves time in the year to teach a few things which are not in the curriculum. They are compelled to do this in order to preserve their own identity. Teachers reduced to robots, because the district curriculum consumes 100 percent of the instructional time, are more likely to be in a career stage other than expert/master teacher.

Curriculum monitoring for the expert/master teacher is self-generated. These teachers are normally exceedingly cognizant of the skills assessed on state tests, national achievement tests, and end-of-year criterion referenced exams. They generally monitor their own instruction to be sure these skills are taught before the tests are administered.

Administrators monitoring curriculum implementation for the expert/master teacher should ascertain that the teacher has the appropriate materials and supplies, as well as assuring that the proper audio visual equipment is available and in good working order. Handling the irate parent, making sure the room is well lit, and occasionally substituting for the teachers, are all ways to support the expert/master's self-generated curriculum monitoring.

Another administrative requirement for this teacher is to show support for the results of his teaching. Attendance at culminating activities is essential, because they provide the benchmarks for progress through the school year. By taking a leisurely walk around the classroom to peruse the student's work one can find ample documentation for the hard work of both the teacher and the students.

Occasionally, the expert/master teacher will redesign a unit of instruction or create a completely new one. When this type of activity is in progress, the administrator can support the teacher's efforts by supplying him with as many resources as possible. Sending a letter on school stationary to other districts in the region that offer instruction in the same field, may generate copies of completed curricular materials which can be modified. Linkages with the major curriculum content associations can be sought. These too, may uncover additional resources. Contacting the curriculum and instruction department of local colleges and universities may also help to produce resources for the teacher.

REWARD STRUCTURE

Teacher reward, which can take almost any form, is the fuel which keeps the expert/master teachers' fires burning brightly. Without it, the career stage cannot be maintained indefinitely.

Teacher burnout is the result of defeated idealism. Burnout cannot happen if there is nothing to burn out. As defined by Pines, Aronson, and Kafry (1981, p. 15), "burnout is the result of constant or repeated emotional pressure associated with an intense involvement with people over long periods of time." There are three components of burnout: physical exhaustion, emotional exhaustion, and mental exhaustion.

The reward structure for teachers at any career stage must eliminate potential sources of burnout. Effective teacher reward must specifically address the teacher, occur immediately after an event, benefit the receiver, be more positive than negative, and be based on actions and on verifiable behavior (Blanchard, 1986).

Phrases like "You know we appreciate what you do" or "We have lots of expert/master teachers in this district" or "This is an excellent school system" are not considered to be specific rewards for teachers. A specific reward can be a letter from the superintendent, a resolution from the board of education, an article in the local newspaper, or a thank-you note from a parent. Whatever form it takes, there should be a connection between the reward and the action of the teacher.

To be most effective, a reward should be closely related to the event for which it is being given. Board acknowledgement of winning the state basketball championship two months after the event is not as significant as noting the event a few days after it happens.

In the mind of the teacher, the reward needs to be linked to specific action taken by her. For example, a reward for volunteering to work with the debate team three nights a week is more meaningful than a reward for being a giving teacher.

The reward should benefit the receiver. A reserved parking spot would have little meaning to the teacher who walks to work each day. But for the teacher who travels a long distance and is sometimes caught in bad traffic jams, a reserved parking spot would be a meaningful reward.

Rewards have to be perceived as more positive than negative. Attendance at a conference may be a positive reward for a teacher, but if the conference coincides with a critical event in the teacher's life, it may turn out to be negative. Administrators should have frank discussions with staff members about rewards. For example, solving the heating and cooling problems in the west wing of the middle school may be a significant reward for some staff members; others may require something more personal.

Finally, the behavior for which the reward is given should be verifiable. That means it is something that can be seen by more than one person. Another administrator should be able to walk into a building and clearly see the indicators of achievement which were the basis for granting the reward.

Due to the nature of the teaching profession and the contracts which regulate teacher payment schedules, increasing a teacher's salary is typically not a decision which can be made by an individual administrator. Most contract pay scales are based on years of education and number of years of service. The teacher's career stage has nothing to do with the pay she receives. The expert/master teacher and the teacher in deep withdrawal with master's degrees and fifteen years of service receive the same pay. The career ladder and merit pay programs now being implemented in more than fifteen states and being considered by many more are intended to "encourage teachers currently employed in the public school system to continue to pursue excellence within their profession, to provide incentives to teachers of demonstrated ability and expertise to remain in the public school system, and to restore the teaching profession to its position of primary importance within the structure of the state educational system" (California State Bill 813).

Few would argue with the objective. However, the plans being designed to achieve the objective tend to offer too little money, specify a limited number of teachers who may receive the money, and establish criteria for achieving the designation that is based to some extent on years of service and level of education. The two critical problems facing the profession are attracting the brightest and best to the field, and retaining expert/master teachers. Many of the plans currently in place do not solve these two problems.

A solution must be found. John Goodlad (1984, p. 313) states that unless we solve these problems, "We might as well resign ourselves to a permanent state of low pay for teachers and the continuation of teaching as a marginal profession." Legislation by state departments can be useful in solving the first problem by attracting the brightest and the best through public relations campaigns, paid scholarships, and financial support for higher minimum salaries. State legislated plans to identify and reward expert/master teachers are frequently complicated, cumbersome, and not very practical. The legislatures, by developing career ladders and merit pay plans, are attempting to do what should be done at the local level, namely to develop a way to reward teachers intrinsically and extrinsically, which supports the growth and maintenance of master/expert teachers. It is a difficult task for a trained professional educator, an impossible one for a layperson without intensive reading.

The possibilities for meaningful reward are limitless. The problem lies in matching the right reward with the right expert/master teacher.

An article appearing in the *Journal of Educational Public Relations* lists close to a hundred ways of rewarding staff. It is interesting that the list was generated as a result of a survey of members of the Pennsylvania and National School Public Relations associations, and a workshop involving administrators in a Pennsylvania school district. The point is that identifying the rewards is not the difficulty—providing the match is. By using the career stages model, administrators can begin to systematically develop reward programs that are valued, meaningful, and which are effective in sustaining teachers at the expert/master teacher stage.

SUMMARY

Expert/master teachers are the shining beacons of excellence in an otherwise endless sea of toiling teachers, many of whom could become such paragons, but do not, because of a lack of understanding, support, and reinforcement by boards of education, the public, school administrators and supervisors.

The number of possible expert/master teachers is not limited. The teacher population is not governed by a bell-shaped curve that forever limits the cadre to only 5 to 10 percent of its total membership. My guess is that 60 to 70 percent of the current teachers could become expert/master teachers if nurtured properly. That estimate is based on my years of experience as a school administrator in three different states, and work with teachers in every kind of setting: urban, suburban, and rural.

It is a myth that the teaching profession is peopled with droves of mediocre pedagogs. The same kind of myth also says that only some children can learn in schools. These myths reflect current school practices which leave much to be desired on many levels. My optimism is not anchored to the present, but rather to our potential as teachers. Believing we can be better is the first step to becoming better. It is time to take that first step.

INQUIRY

Questions and Answers About Chapter Four

Question #1: *Are there any promising research trends to identify expert/master teachers in the schools?*

Answer: Most definitely. I see researchers abandoning descriptive studies and moving to understanding how teachers define excellence in the language they use. The point of view is being changed from so-called objective observer to participant observer. I think this is promising.

Question #2: *Can it be correctly assumed that while an expert/master teacher has many incentives to remain at this stage it cannot be guaranteed that he/she, in fact, will remain there?*

Answer: Correct. An expert/master teacher must be nurtured, supported, reinforced like anyone else. Even the most independent ones I know appreciate knowledgeable praise of their work.

Question #3: *What's the most potent strategy for developing and keeping expert/master teachers?*

Answer: Recognizing them first, finding ways to acknowledge their importance, and using tangible and visible means of supporting their work. The bottom line is to capitalize upon the intrinsic motivators.

Question #4: *What about career ladders? Aren't they supposed to do just that?*

Answer: In theory, that is what a lot of career ladders are about. In practice, I see too many mired in existing traditions. Perhaps the most fatal flaw of all is that the expert/master teacher wants to work a longer work year to make more money. Teaching is an exhausting activity. More than many other teachers, the expert/master teacher must have time to recharge the batteries.

Question #5: *What about merit pay?*

Answer: My experience with expert/master teachers indicates that many would avoid merit pay. Remember, while teachers expect to be paid well, they didn't enter teaching purely for money. So money can't be used as the primary motivator. Also, most merit amounts are so small they are not worth the administrative time used to justify their application in the schools.

REFERENCES

American Association of School Administrators. *Effective Teaching, Observations from Research*. Arlington, Virginia (1986).

BLANCHARD, M. *Human Development* (1986).

BLOOM, B. et al. *Taxonomy of Educational Objectives: Handbook I: Cognitive Domain*. New York:David McKay Company (1956).

DARROW, C. *The Story of My Life*. New York:Grosset and Dunlap (1932).

GAZDA, G. *Human Relations Development, Manual for Educators*. Boston: Allyn and Bacon, Inc. (1973).

GOODLAD, J. *A Place Called School*. New York:McGraw-Hill (1984).

HUNTER, M. *Mastery Teaching*. El Segundo, California:TIP Publications (1982).

JOYCE, B. *Improving American Schools*. New York:Longman (1983).

KARPINSKI, J. "Recognizing the Achievements of Your Staff." *Journal of Educational Public Relations* (Spring, 1985).

PARSONS, C. *Seeds: Some Good Ways to Improve on Schools*. Santa Barbara, California:Woodbridge Press (1985).

PINES, A., E. Aronson and D. Kafry. *Burnout*. New York:The Free Press (1981).

SCOPES, J. *Center of the Storm*. New York:Holt, Reinhart, Winston (1967).

TABA, H. *Curriculum Development*. New York:Harcourt, Brace and World (1962).

The renewal stage.

chapter
_____
FIVE

The Renewal Stage

CHARACTERISTICS OF TEACHERS IN RENEWAL

RENEWAL is a form of rebirth. It denotes a time of increased energy, a positive attitude, and a period of growth. Renewal is marked by the intensity of feelings and perception, and by the internal awareness of change. One becomes in tune with one's senses and risk-taking behavior is attempted. In a different sort of way it is like being in love during the social ritual of courtship.

The stage of renewal for a classroom teacher normally involves one or all of the following characteristics.

Conceptual Clarity

A teacher in renewal has invented, created, or discovered new reasons for a recommitment of time and energy to teaching. A good illustration of this was the closing scene in the movie *Teachers* starring Nick Nolte. In that scene a fire drill, during which students were milling about on the front steps of the high school, has occurred and Nolte is being berated. When he is challenged about the fact that half the students who went out to the fire drill won't come back and that he is crazy to care about them, he answers with a shrug, "I'm a teacher."

The film is about Nolte's own regeneration. He once had a reputation for being an outstanding teacher, but he slipped and fell into withdrawal. But the events in the movie regenerate his dedication to his profession and he starts again. The law suit brought by a former student in the school, and the female lawyer representing the plaintiff, who was once Nolte's student, first produce turmoil, and

83

then a new conceptual clarity of why he cares at all about continuing to teach.

Emotional Tension

Renewed teachers are emotional. They are passionate about what drives them and in what they believe. This focus provides the enthusiasm they are able to project. They are like terrible poker players who have a great hand and can't bluff anybody about what they have. They are exuberant. Don't misunderstand me, they are not foaming at the mouth or nervous like the teacher in the anticipatory stage may be; rather, they are quietly but noticeably emotional about their teaching. Students can recognize this almost immediately. The tension is detectable and, when it involves sound planning and conceptual clarity, it is very much like a kind of music that can lift the soul, sweep away barriers of time and space, and move even the most reluctant learner. The teachers who move their students in this way are most often in the act of renewal.

Sustained High-Energy Thrust

The teacher in the renewal stage is capable of long periods of sustained high energy. Halpin and Croft (1963), although they were talking about a behavior of school leaders, have called this period of sustained high energy "thrust." The same characteristic is common among teachers in renewal and it permeates everything they do. Such teachers come early and stay late. They never stop thinking about the job. They are like a football coach drawing "x's" and "o's" on his napkin because he's always thinking about the game and about plays that will make his team more formidable and effective.

Teachers in renewal can't easily separate work and play. For them, both are the same. Teachers in renewal are always working. They seem to have discoverd a fountain or a vitamin pill that results in incredible bursts of high energy over periods of time.

Realism and Humor

Teachers in renewal are, unlike their inexperienced pedagogical colleagues at the anticipatory stage, realistic about what they can do and what students can do. They have a higher level of realistic aspirations than many of their colleagues do about the same students.

Teachers in renewal are zealous but not humorless. They aren't so filled with their own importance that they can't find perspective in their work, and that means they have a sense of humor about themselves, about their own foibles, and about humanity. That is what I call realism. Yet this realism is the practical result of tempering the steel of idealism. Teachers in renewal believe they make a difference. They believe in their influence as teachers—as human beings capable of touching other human beings and, as a result of their work, capable of changing the human condition. They are patient with humanity, but impatient with the conditions that strangle humanity in prejudice, ignorance, and intolerance.

Skill

Teachers in renewal are skillful, because they have mastered the basic moves of teaching and can improvise. They can create a thousand different rhythms in a classroom with everyone keeping the same beat. Like great athletes, they make complex moves look simple.

Drama

Teachers in the renewal stage forget the niceties of role and title. They are often swept up by the force of their own enthusiasm. They can rhapsodize eloquently as to how Alexander the Great led his troops over the wall first, daring the enemy to take him on, or understand the intricacies of T. S. Eliot's poetry or appreciate the fact that great mathematical ideas are essentially pretty.

The persona of a teacher in renewal is inextricably linked to his or her character. In such teachers there is a kind of presence that produces a reverence from students who intuitively grasp that someone special is in their midst.

Inquisitiveness

Teachers in renewal have opened up their minds and are looking for answers. They have set aside their former "forcefields" (Lewin, 1936) and are open to new ones being reformulated. Teachers in renewal are curious. They are observers again, looking at the same but new phenomenon. In so doing, they challenge their own familiarity with events. In the process of re-examination, they see again with new eyes, just like the first time they saw something that inspired

them. They are like farmers who find every spring filled with the
same promise as the first one.

Naiveté

Teachers in renewal live in a state of suspended naiveté. While
they know that everyting doesn't always work out, that the schools
they work in are often detrimental to the development of the
children they were built to serve, that the community may be ig-
norant or unappreciative of their labors, and that the principal may
be a nitpicker or a compulsive rule-aholic, they can suspend all of
that when they enter their classrooms. The classroom is their stage
and the world is displayed on it. Teachers in renewal are wonderfully
naive. However, this is due to carefully controlled contrivance,
designed to protect them from the realities that, if allowed, would
crush them.

In this sense, teachers in renewal are childlike. They shut out the
world and teach. Teachers in renewal are the Peter Pans in our
schools. The rest may see drudgery, sterility, and evil. Teachers in renewal never lose their wonder of the world. The rest may curse it, de-
spise it, loathe it; teachers in renewal revel in it. They are the
candles that burn in the cold churches at night. They are the light
in the darkness. They are the ones that hear every parent's prayers
when they send their children to school all over the world. The problem is that there are too few of them. The task of the school administration is to take the conditions that create renewal and enhance
them, thereby increasing the number of teachers in renewal. This
process will lead to the spiritual regeneration of the school itself.
That is called enshrining the multiplier effect.

Some teachers are able to create the conditions within schools and
within their classrooms by which they recycle themselves through
renewal throughout their careers. Such teachers are rare, but every
school building has at least one or two. These teachers are comfortable being alone. They are like Abraham Lincoln taking long walks
in the woods by himself. They are self-supporting, nearly autonomous. They find the pleasures of renewal rewarding in and of itself
and require little formal recognition or encouragement.

But the Abraham Lincolns of the world are few and far between.
For schools to create a "critical mass" of teachers able to generate
sufficient energy to engage in institutional renewal, working conditions have to be created so that many teachers are simultaneously

engaged in career renewal. That is the job of the school administration.

RELATING PERKS TO TEACHER RENEWAL

Most teachers will require help. They need the assistance of a caring, sensitive, and supportive administrator. Blanchard and Tager (1986) have identified five PERKS which, when present in an organization, help people enter renewal and by so doing, maintain themselves at the expert/master teacher stage of the career stages model. The PERKS are:

P = participation
E = environment
R = recognition
K = knowledge
S = style

The administrator attempting to maintain a high level of renewal within the system must consider how these PERKS are being delivered.

The key to renewal is the individual teacher's perception of how the organization views the individual. If the teacher feels the organization does not value him, doesn't really care one way or the other, or has a negative view of what he brings to the organization, then renewal is not possible. The only consequence for the teacher is to exit the system or withdrawal.

Most teachers do not get up in the morning and consciously decide not to do a good job on any given day. Most believe they do a good job, given the constraints of the system. However, when the teacher believes he can't do a good job because of the system's constraints, he is in withdrawal. The teacher's perception of organizational constraints is an indicator of withdrawal.

When asked to place themselves in a career stage, and the choices do not include an average or satisfactory category, many teachers place themselves in the withdrawal stage. However, they quickly follow with a litany of reasons why they are in withdrawal. The vast majority of these reasons relate to deficiencies in the "PERKS" of the organization.

Since it is the role of the administration to create a climate where attention is paid to each of these PERKS, the climate for renewal within the organization is often directly related to the competency of the administration.

Administrators are the catalysts, and the teachers are the elements of renewal. The equation isn't balanced without both. The product of system renewal will not be generated without the catalyst. The issue is very complex.

Participation

Asking for someone's opinion changes that person from a passive observer to an active participant. The teacher actively involved in the work environment is one who generally contributes to that environment in some way. It can be a negative or a positive involvement. Either way, there is action.

The first step toward renewal is to get a teacher interested in some new program, technique, idea, or innovation. Renewal cannot be mandated. It requires the personal commitment of the teacher, the desire to explore, to seek out, to stretch, and to grow.

For the administrator, it requires a basic belief in the goodness of mankind, the theory approach to people (McGregor, 1960). "Too many managers treat employees like children—and then are surprised when they behave like children" (Peters and Waterman, 1982). Sometimes administrators get so involved in the day-to-day activities of running the organization, they forget or don't think they have the time to involve their staff in decisions that affect them.

The teacher in renewal is trying to improve something, which will ultimately result in students being able to improve something.

Getting the teacher's attention and interest can begin by involving her in the day-to-day decision making of the organization. All organizations face daily challenges. Involving teachers in finding solutions to the problems confronting the organization may be a first step to renewal, because the problems are no longer the organization's problems; rather the individual teachers have a stake in them and begin to "own them." With the ownership comes the desire to solve the problem, to accept the challenge to change.

This type of participation requires a collegial working relationship, in which it is "okay" to talk honestly to the boss. Administrators can encourage this type of relationship with their staff through their body language, eye contact, and gestures. The nonverbal language of acceptance is a universal language, that is immediately understood by old and young alike.

Involving teachers in decision making regarding their content area or grade level is one way of encouraging participation. The development of Subject Advisory Committees which meet regularly to improve a content area is an effective way to realize that involvement. These committees can be chaired by teachers, department chairpersons, or supervisors. They work best when they have clearly defined decision-making powers. They should be voluntary, have yearly agendas, and meet on a regular basis.

Environment

An environment rich in opportunities for growth supports renewal. In-service programs are based on teachers' interests, professional journals and books are supplied by the district, and conference and workshop attendance is encouraged. This is an environment in which the district expects continued professional growth. Sabbaticals and tuition reimbursement are common in districts with a growth-oriented environment. These districts actively solicit funds to support renewal efforts. Although the amount of money generated by these grants is often small, the effect on the system can be pervasive. Good begets good. Grants often bring in other funds. Once a central idea or growth area has been identified for a content area, system, or building, then the administrator can begin to infuse the system with resources in that area. Speakers, materials, books, and ideas, all focusing on a central theme, begin to generate synergy within the system. More and more people begin to get interested in the concept. If supported, encouraged, and promoted, the programs can become a signal for renewal.

All of this assumes that the environment is one which supports solid classroom performance. This means that the necessary materials and supplies to deliver instruction are readily available. It means classrooms are adequately furnished, lit, and ventilated. It means a class size that is appropriate for the grade level and type of student. Like Maslow's (1954) hierarchy, self-actualization is not possible unless the physical and safety needs of the individuals are met. Renewal is not possible unless the environment supports it.

Recognition

Everyone likes recognition. It feels good. However, recognition has to be given in such a way that it does not make us look like braggarts. Feedback is the core of recognition and may be given to a teacher in a multitude of ways, but it always means letting the teacher know how she is doing. No feedback means no recognition. No recognition means no reward, and no reward over a long period of time means courting withdrawal.

Often an administrator will assume that teachers perceive the absence of negative comments as positive reward. Wrong! Neutral or no feedback is almost always perceived by the teacher as negative. Administrators fail to realize that when they say nothing to a teacher, the teacher perceives this as negative reinforcement. Add to this the negative comments that are made to teachers regarding what they should or shouldn't do, and one has a situation in which a large proportion of the communication going out into the system is being interpreted as negative.

For feedback to be perceived as a positive reward, it must be directed to a specific behavior, occur within a time period closely linked to the event, contain more positive than negative information, and be presented in a way that is not repetitious of the last situation for which the individual received feedback.

In order to deliver this type of feedback, the administrator has to be in tune with the staff. He must know each one and what he is doing well in order to be able to deliver specific feedback. Telling a teacher that you like what she does is all well and good, but it isn't enough. Telling her that the unit she prepared using the integrated language arts approach was effective, based on the quality of the student writing displayed in the room, is far more meaningful to the teacher.

Knowledge

Two of the new "buzz words" in the profession today are vision and mission. They are important words. They speak to the future oriented behavior of administrators. Vision implies that the administrator can see into the future and can see where the district, building, or department should be going in order to meet the needs of students who will become functioning adults around the year 2000. Mission implies that the administrator can translate that vision into the pragmatics of a long-range plan and yearly goals.

Assuming the administrator has the competency to do both, it is important for the staff to know what the vision and mission are, and how the district intends to achieve them. It has been said that knowledge is power, and that is true. The power of shared knowledge and commitment within an organization is the power that fuels renewal.

Teachers work in isolation. They rarely attend board meetings and do not attend central office meetings. They rarely attend cross-grade-level or cross-department meetings. It is not unusual for a group of elementary teachers to come together at a grade-level meeting and not know one another even though they have worked for the same system for many years.

It is incorrect to assume that the science department at the high school knows what is going on in science instruction at the elementary level. This is the exception rather than the rule.

It is up to the central administration to ensure that the goals and objectives of the organization are shared, understood, and accepted. Progress toward goals must be communicated to the staff periodically in order to provide them with the necessary feedback to help the district progress. Sometimes administrators withhold information or share it in bits and pieces, using it to maintain their own feelings of power. In doing so, they damage the system and inhibit renewal.

The practice of asking teachers to set goals is not new. Management by objectives has been around for a long time, but it fails as a vehicle for staff renewal when the teacher sees no relationship between what he sets as goals and where the district is headed (see Dreeben, 1973). Management by objectives is very often seen as a paper process and many times it is just that. However, if the teachers can see how their work is combining with the work of other professional staff persons to help children grow and the system improve, they will work harder to help achieve the stated objectives.

Style

It has long been recognized that there is no type of leadership style that is appropriate for all people in all situations. Bennis and Nanus (1985) discuss the complexity of leadership today. While gathering information for their book, they interviewed a number of chief executive officers of successful public and private organizations all over the United States. They found autocratic leaders and democratic leaders, college educated leaders and high school dropouts, male and female leaders, tall leaders and short leaders, articulate and inarticulate leaders. They discovered that all of the successful leaders they interviewed had in common the ability to give the organization a vision for what it could be, and the ability to activate the resources of the system to make that vision a reality.

That means working with a wide variety of people who are at

different places in their own professional and personal development, being able to instill in those people the desire to work to transform the mission of the organization into reality. Sometimes that involves directing the behavior of subordinates; sometimes that means coaching. Occasionally it means delegating and often it means supporting behavior. It denotes being flexible and sensitive. It means being there during success and failure. It means sometimes being a friend, a colleague, or a peer. It means being many different things to many different people.

IN-SERVICE FOR THE TEACHER IN RENEWAL

The teacher in renewal has made a commitment to growth. He could be classified as an enthusiastic beginner, because in many ways he resembles the teacher at the anticipatory stage. He feels a new surge of professional energy moving through his veins. The biggest difference between the anticipatory teacher and the teacher in renewal is the source of motivation. The anticipatory teacher is excited about everything. The teacher in renewal has channeled his motivation toward a specific skill, body of knowledge, program, or activity.

In-service for the teacher in renewal must be directed to his area of interest and be ongoing. Sometimes it is possible to get a group of teachers together who share a common area of interest. Perhaps they are all interested in helping the district develop a student assistance program. Or maybe they are interested in creating a program to enhance student critical thinking skills. If this is the case, it is important for the district to provide the in-service at the local level. As they work together, the teachers will begin to develop their own professional support group. An administrator should be assigned to orchestrate the development and implementation of the program. The development of the program should become part of the district's long-range plan, and budget considerations should be given to the program. The fact that the program is being developed should be shared internally with staff and be the basis of district news releases.

In-service activities to support the program should extend over a long period of time. After the teacher in renewal experiences the excitement and exhilaration of learning about a new venture, a period of disillusionment occurs. This is a crucial time, and unless the teacher receives the attention, encouragement, and support he needs, he is likely to reject the whole idea and fall quickly into withdrawal. If the area of renewal is limited to the individual teacher, it is often more difficult to provide the time, attention, and in-service support needed to have the teacher succeed. In-service for this type of renewal must be sought out. Often it will take place at workshops outside the district where connections with other districts or with businesses will be made. Sometimes it requires a liaison with a local university. When a teacher has identified an area in which he wants to grow, then it becomes the responsibility of the administrator to seek out resources to support that renewal.

An administrator can begin by developing a file of innovative ideas, programs, research summaries, area experts, national contacts, and association data to support renewal efforts. Once an area of renewal has been identified, the administrator should be looking for information to share with the teacher. This not only helps the teacher continue to grow, but also helps to provide him with necessary support to prevent the renewing teacher from becoming a disillusioned learner.

SUPERVISION OF THE TEACHER IN RENEWAL

Supervising the teacher in renewal is an individualized process. Whatever the district's formal procedures, they will be ineffective in maintaining and supporting the growth process. The teacher in renewal needs a cheerleader, and the administrator to whom she reports is in the best position to perform that role. Like the children's story, *The Little Engine that Could,* the teacher has to be told again and again, "You can do it, you can do it, you can do it."

When the teacher is beginning to try out some of the ideas that were learned during the in-service, she should know that the administrator does not expect perfection with the first try. We usually understand that, with children, learning a new skill is not easy; but when it comes to an adult's growth, we somehow expect instant competence.

Trying out a new skill with twenty-five observers watching requires a strong self-concept. Children know when the teachers are struggling and so do the teachers themselves. The school climate has to be such that taking risks and failing is okay. If the classroom and school environments are trusting ones, and the support for renewal is strong, students, teachers, and administrators will grow in their respect for one another.

In the initial stages of testing the idea, the supervisory behavior of the administrator should be low-keyed and informal. Occasional visits before or after school just to chat with the teacher are encouraged. This lets the teacher know that the administrator is interested in what she is doing, but that he is not there to judge how well it is being done. It also helps to build the informal rapport that is necessary to support new learning and growth.

When the teacher is ready for more formal feedback, she should ask for it and specify exactly what form it should take. This may require for the administrator to learn some new observation techniques. The teacher may want the administrator to focus only on the questions that the students ask, or the level of *Bloom's Taxonomy* (1956), addressed by the student's questions. Or the teacher may want the administrator to provide feedback regarding the percent of teacher talk versus student talk. The teacher may want the administrator to evaluate the learning climate of the room or to focus on one student's or a small group of student's behavior. It is important to remember that the administrator should be viewed as someone who will supply the teacher with information which in turn will enable the teacher to grow.

Video should not be overlooked as a means of providing the teacher with additional feedback. The days have passed when everyone stiffened at the sight of a video camera; now they are considered commonplace additions to the classroom. A video camera can be placed in a classroom such that with a few simple operations, the teacher can turn it on, tape, review what has been recorded, and erase the sequence. With each camera that is purchased, the district has the potential for expanding its capability to provide feedback to teachers. If the basic assumption that teachers desire to do a good job is correct, and I believe it is, then it follows that teachers may be the best judges of their own behavior, and the best source of feedback for themselves.

CURRICULUM MONITORING OF THE TEACHER IN RENEWAL

Very often, renewal causes the curriculum of the grade level or subject to be changed, and the administration should support and promote this effort in the best way possible. This could mean that the district would contract with an expert in the field to review the curriculum being developed. Given the fact that there are over 15,000 school districts in the United States, it is inconceivable that there is a topic for which some district has not developed a curriculum. Add to that the plethora of private businesses which continue to develop curricula for schools, and one has an enormous resource available to districts. It truly is not necessary to reinvent the wheel. Although each curriculum guide would have to be modified to fit the particular needs of a district, the beginnings of that guide are already available. It would be advantageous for professional organizations to begin to solicit these guides and act as a clearing house for their dissemination. Until this happens, it may be necessary for the districts to solicit the available guides and buy them. The point here is that the teacher should receive the benefit of whatever curricular support the administration can provide. If the renewal area requires the development of new material, the district should consider eliminating the teacher's duty assignment. Curriculum development takes time, and to expect a teacher to do it after school or during her free time is absurd. When more than one teacher is interested in new curriculum for a given content area, a team of teachers may be selected to do the development work. This provides the teachers with both help in the development process and a support group.

Curriculum development does not have to be confined to one district. Neighboring districts with similar student populations would benefit by cooperatively working together in the curriculum development process. It may even facilitate the renewal process by encouraging cross-district peer consultations.

REWARD STRUCTURE

For this stage as for many of the others, the best reward is the administrator's personal time and attention. Beyond that, the teacher in renewal should be recognized for the extra time and effort she has put forth to improve the educational program. This recognition can take the form of articles in the district newsletter, presentations at PTA meetings, and culminating activities to which parents and community are invited.

One of the best rewards any teacher can get is to have her students tell her that they like her work, and that they appreciate the extra effort the teacher has made to help them. Student opinion polls can be employed for this feedback to teachers. Again, this can be done in such a way that the teacher is the only one to see the data. Districts spend a lot of time ensuring that students are recognized for their work; perhaps the district administration can work with the teachers union to design ways for teachers to be rewarded for their work as well.

SUMMARY

The renewal stage is not a state, it is a process. Instead of being a noun, it is a verb. It is "becoming." Once a teacher thinks she is in renewal she probably is. Renewal is the process of reaching, growing, trying, risking, thinking, and improving. It is very much an action verb. One never gets there. It's the "going" that counts. Thus renewal is transition. To be most useful to a school or a school system, renewal has to be guided so that it reinforces what the school and the system are about. That is the function of the school administration.

By its very nature, renewal is collegial and participative. Bystanders and observers are not committed to the hard work of change. To change, to take the chance of failure, a support system must be present. Only in a positive school climate where the professional and personal risks are minimized, can renewal become a reality.

INQUIRY

Questions and Answers About Chapter Five

Question #1: *How do teachers respond to the idea of renewal when you've presented it to them? Do they believe it? Do cynics among them have a field day?*

Answer: Response to the model has been quite positive. Teachers have told me that it's the first time someone has presented a model to them with which they can identify. Of course, it is viewed as simplistic in that everyone agrees that you can't place people in little boxes and label them. However, the overall behavior and attitude of teachers does allow for differentiation. For some, especially those who viewed themselves as expert/master teachers and know that something within them is changing, it helps to clarify what may be happening to them and why. Those in withdrawal, to date, have not identified themselves to me and argued negatively about the model. To do that is to admit at least entering withdrawal. The model seems to give administrators some food for thought. Some are anxious to share the model with their staff, others want to use it to redesign staff development programs. Union representatives haven't taken issue with it yet, but I'm sure that they would, if by implementing the model, staff members were publicly identified as being in withdrawal. We have a hard enough time trying to get support for recognizing exemplary teacher behavior, let alone unexemplary behavior. I suspect, anticipatory, expert/master teachers, and those in renewal will like it. The exit teacher probably won't care and the teacher in withdrawal will voice severe criticism.

Question #2: *Do teacher associations or unions find anything objectionable in the school administration's efforts to engage teachers as a group in renewal?*

Answer: Like so many things in school environments, it depends on the level of trust and respect that exists between the union and the administration. If the administration is perceived as hard-nosed, authoritative, and not responsive to or caring for teachers, attempts to engage teachers in renewal will be looked upon with suspicion. There will be allegations that the model is an attempt at removing tenure. The flags will wave and the efforts will be sabotaged. On the other hand, if the trust factor is strong, the union and associations will be supportive. They are just as interested in teacher renewal as the administration is, maybe more so. Implementation of any aspect of the model should be done in a cooperative way. Union and association building representatives should understand what the administration is attempting to do to support renewal and why.

Question #3: *Are there any "no-no's" for the board or administration to consider when initiating efforts at renewal?*

Answer: Yes. Don't make it a big deal. This is not a program of which the public needs to be informed in the district's newsletter. It works best when it is done quietly. The less often the words "in renewal" are used, the better. The program would be defeated if the public thought that administrators were labeling teachers. Every parent would demand his/her child to be taught by a teacher in renewal, or at the expert/master teacher level.

Question #4: *If renewal is not permanent, how does the administrator maintain the cycle?*

Answer: By continuing to be sensitive to the behavior changes in the staff, so that early signs of withdrawal are noted and attention is given to the teacher to bring him/her back into the cycle.

REFERENCES

BENNIS, W. and B. Nanus. *Leaders—Strategies for Taking Charge.* New York:Harper and Row (1985).

BLANCHARD, M. and M. Tager. *Working Well.* New York:Simon and Schuster (1986).

BLOOM, B. et al. *Taxonomy of Educational Objectives: Handbook I, The Cognitive Domain.* New York:David McKay Company, Inc. (1956).

DREEBEN, R. "The School as a Workplace." In *Second Handbook of Research on Teaching,* R. Travers, ed. Chicago:Rand McNally & Company, pp. 450–473 (1973).

HALPIN, A. and D. Croft. *The Organizational Climate of Schools.* Chicago:University of Chicago, Midwest Administration Center (1963).

MASLOW, A. *Motivation and Personality.* New York:Harper and Row (1954).

McGREGOR, D. *The Human Side of Enterprise.* New York:McGraw-Hill (1960).

PETERS, T. and R. Waterman. *In Search of Excellence.* New York:Harper and Row (1982).

The withdrawal stage.

chapter
_____
SIX

The Withdrawal Stage

A NEGATIVE FORCE IN THE SYSTEM

THE teacher in withdrawal represents a negative force in the system. The ability of the system to grow, to improve, and to change is inversely related to the percentage of teachers in withdrawal and the level of their withdrawal. Three levels of withdrawal can be identified:

—initial withdrawal
—persistent withdrawal
—deep withdrawal

The vast majority of teachers in withdrawal are in the initial withdrawal stage. These are the teachers who, for one reason or another, have begun to detach themselves from the system. Without intervention, they may move to the level of persistent withdrawal and finally into deep withdrawal. It is almost impossible to bring a teacher out of deep withdrawal. Typically, they leave the system on a medical disability related to physical or mental deterioration, they voluntarily retire from the system bitter and beaten, or there is some type of buy-out resulting in a resignation.

CHARACTERISTICS OF THE TEACHER IN WITHDRAWAL

Withdrawal is characterized by various degrees of physical, emotional, and mental exhaustion. The teacher in withdrawal exhibits a loss of physical energy. He has a sense of helplessness and hopelessness and experiences constant emotional drain. He has a low self-concept and a pervasive negative attitude toward students, administration, work, and life in general. The teacher believes that he is no longer in control of his life. Professional goal-setting has ceased and he has a general feeling of distress, anxiety, frustration, anger, and discontent. The teacher in the withdrawal stage experiences a combination of burnout and tedium.

Tedium and burnout are related but different states. They frequently result in the same observable behavior, but the source of the behavior is different (Pines, Aronson, and Kafry, 1981, p. 15). "Tedium can be the result of any prolonged chronic pressure (mental, physical, or emotional)." A teacher who experiences a heart attack followed by a long period of recovery may be the victim of tedium. A teacher who has been the target of continued parental pressure over a sustained period of time may also qualify. In addition, the teacher who is under severe emotional stress because of a loved one's illness can begin to move from a previous state of renewal into withdrawal.

Pines, Aronson, and Kafry (1981) also noted, "Burnout is the result of constant or repeated emotional pressure associated with an intense involvement with people over long periods of time." Burnout happens because of the teacher's interaction with the children. Tedium, on the other hand, occurs for different reasons but is exhibited by the teacher in much the same way. Burnout frequently happens in the helping professions and particularly in teaching when the teacher comes to believe that he cannot teach in a way that the students will learn. These teachers feel they have nothing left to give.

Burnout and tedium are difficult to separate and often go hand in hand. Together, they form the basis for the career stage of teacher withdrawal.

The vast majority of teachers working in our schools today alternate between a state of renewal and a state of withdrawal. The stage the teacher is in is often related to the number and frequency of positive and negative experiences he encounters in the day-to-day work environment. When the number and frequency of negative experiences exceeds that of positive experiences, the teacher moves from renewal to withdrawal.

By understanding the causes and recognizing the behavioral signs, an administrator or the teacher himself may be able to change the work environment or modify the outside environment in order to reverse the situation and place the teacher back into a state of renewal.

According to Pines, Aronson, and Kafry (1981, pp. 17–21), specific characteristics associated with tedium and burnout can be observed:

Physical	Emotional	Mental
Low energy	Depression	Negative attitudes
Chronic fatigue	Helplessness	Low self-concept
Weakness	Entrapment	Feeling incompetent
Weariness	Thoughts of suicide	Feeling inferior
Accident-prone	Loss of control and	Pessimistic
Frequent headaches	coping mechanism	Dehumanizing
Frequent illness	Emotional depletion	attitudes towards
Back pain	Irritable	others
Use of alcohol	Nervous	Arrive late, leave
Other chemicals		early
Overeating		Extend breaks
		Lack of concentration
		Blaming attitude

Withdrawal can occur at any time in the life of a professional educator. Few teachers are successful in completing their career without some periods of withdrawal. The occurrence and length of the withdrawal are often related to the extent of the teacher's idealism, the nature of the work environment, and the occurrence of outside events in the life of the professional. The teacher who is most susceptible to withdrawal is the one who entered the field intent on saving the poor, disadvantaged, learning disabled, culturally deprived child—the teacher who is not very interested in the paycheck, but is dedicated to teaching.

Withdrawal is unavoidable. Given the right environmental conditions, almost everyone will go into a state of withdrawal at one time in his career. However, a state of withdrawal that lasts for a long time and becomes a way of life is avoidable. By acknowledging the existence of withdrawal and recognizing the early signs, professionals can learn coping mechanisms which prevent future episodes of withdrawal, or at least reduce their intensity. Educators tend to believe that they alone experience the early feelings of withdrawal. By accepting the feelings and utilizing the support of others to deal with these early signs, persistent and deep withdrawal can be avoided. An administrator trained to identify the early signs of initial withdrawal can intervene and bring that teacher back into the cycle of renewal to master/teacher to renewal.

People who maintain a positive attitude, who seek out opportunities for growth, and who look for the best in a situation, are generally those who are healthy, both physically and mentally. Conversely, those who are quick to point out the errors made by students, administrators, and fellow teachers, who reject change, and who frequently criticize, are often plagued with physical and mental problems. This situation is comparable to the chicken and egg problem: Which came first, the physical and mental problems or the change in attitude? Although there is little definitive research to verify it, the attitude change may precede the physical or mental change. Applied to this model, the teacher begins to slip into initial withdrawal, and then experiences physical or mental problems.

The rapid development of employee assistance programs and our current national awareness of physical fitness are both examples of support for this position. It has been proven that physical activity reduces stress and promotes a positive attitude. Firms that spend considerable amounts of money on employee assistance programs do so because they want to maintain high levels of productivity for their staff.

Unless the administrator is attuned to the climate of the organization and knows each individual staff member well enough to be aware of subtle changes in attitude, he may miss the opportunity to intervene at the onset of withdrawal. The teacher himself may not be completely aware of what is happening.

While withdrawal may take place at any age level, it is more often found in teachers who have been in the system for more than five years. During the first few years in the system, teachers are at the anticipatory stage, learning about the system, the community, and themselves as teachers. After that, they are usually in a stage of renewal leading to the expert/master teacher stage. At some point in the renewal process, the teacher may begin to change direction, moving away from the expert/master teacher stage and beginning to enter withdrawal. Withdrawal does not refer to the day-to-day ups and downs experienced during work; rather, it refers to a prolonged period—a semester or a full year—when the overall behavior of a professional staff person seems to indicate a shift in thrust.

INITIAL WITHDRAWAL

The teacher is the first to know when he begins to enter withdrawal. His energy level begins to drop and he converses less often with colleagues. He may actually begin to move more slowly. He also smiles less frequently. Even his classroom takes on a quiet tone. There is less laughter. His presentations to students become more monotonous. He stops offering suggestions to the administration. He stops asking questions. He becomes neutral. His attitude seems to communicate that, "It really doesn't matter."

Because of system pressures and because many groups demand time, attention and intervention, the teacher slipping into withdrawal can go undetected, even though he may be aware that something has changed. He is often unable to ask for help. Few of us can say, "Stop what you are doing. Listen to me. I'm in trouble here. I need help!" Even if we manage to say this to a peer or a close friend, we often don't know what to do. As a result, nothing is said, the initial level of withdrawal passes, and the teacher moves to persistent withdrawal.

PERSISTENT WITHDRAWAL

The teacher at the level of persistent withdrawal can be characterized as a thorn in the side of the administration. The quiet period has passed and now the teacher is vocal and critical. He is critical about most things: the classes are too large, the students are unprepared, there are too many interruptions, the board is too involved in the administrative affairs of the district, and so on. He is the kind of teacher who can be counted on to take issue with the administration. At a faculty meeting, he is the first to raise his hand to complain, to point out the latest error in thinking made by the administration. Quite often, such teachers hold administrative positions with the union; they like to be part of the negotiating team. They take great pride in maintaining a division between labor and management. They watch the clock and frequently walk out of meetings that exceed the contractual limitations by more than sixty seconds no matter what is being discussed. They like to congregate, and one can often find them in the teachers' room pontificating and plotting during their preparation time.

DEEP WITHDRAWAL

Without administrative intervention, teachers in persistent withdrawal eventually move to the level of deep withdrawal. Although this is another quiet time, this one can be destructive to children, the system, and to the teacher. The teacher in deep withdrawal is commonly referred to as having retired on the job. This is the teacher who takes from the system in the form of monetary compensation, but returns very little in the form of work. Curriculum revisions are ignored, and the district-adopted curriculum is not used to plan instruction. Lesson plans, if there are any, are the same ones that have been used for the past five years. These teachers are frequently among the last to arrive and the first to leave. They neither participate in co-curricular activities as advisers or coaches, nor do they attend school functions. They often have a business on the side or an avocation that consumes most of their creative energies. They view their position as teachers as a job that offers them continued compensation and the prospects of a generous retirement, while enabling them to pursue other interests. If not involved in a side venture, these teachers may have severe and debilitating physical or mental problems.

When a system attempts to remove tenure, it is almost always from a teacher in deep withdrawal. Since the attempt is usually fruitless, the damage to the climate of the entire system is rarely worth the effort involved. The percentage of cases where this type of litigation has been successful is exceedingly small. The work is time-consuming and ugly, and quite often puts the administrator charged with the responsibility of collecting the data into withdrawal.

IDENTIFYING TEACHERS AT THE BEGINNING STAGES OF WITHDRAWAL

Periodically, a building administrator should reflect on each professional in the building. These questions should guide his thought processes.

How well do I know the teacher, personally and professionally?

Is the teacher experiencing a personal crisis at this time? If so, what is the nature of the crisis and what assistance is the teacher receiving?

What kind of support group does the teacher have among other faculty members?

Is the teacher involved in any new, innovative programs within the district?

Does the teacher participate in any co-curricular activities within the district?

How long has the teacher been working in the field of education?

When was the last time I had an informal conversation with the teacher?

Has the teacher attended any workshops or conferences in the past two years?

Has the teacher requested any new materials or equipment?

When was the last time the teacher enrolled in a college course?

Has the teacher filed a grievance?

During the past year, what types of comments has this teacher generally made at faculty meetings?

Is this teacher one with whom you share new ideas?

With this information, it should be relatively easy for an administrator to identify staff persons who are exhibiting changes in their behavior which may indicate that they are beginning to withdraw from the system. If the change in behavior is the result of events in the personal life of the staff member (for example, a family member contracting cancer, or a divorce), he then needs support from the system. If the support is not forthcoming, the withdrawal process begins. The teacher will then say, "You didn't care about me when I was experiencing this problem, so I don't care about you now." This is not a childish reaction; it is a human reaction.

PREVENTATIVE ACTIONS TO AVOID WITHDRAWAL

While the in-service suggestions described here may be helpful for any teacher in withdrawal, they are particularly useful for the teacher in the beginning stages of withdrawal. No one wants to go into withdrawal, and the individual approaching it may not know what is happening. The system must have mechanisms in place to help the teacher. One such mechanism is a staff assistance program. Most of these programs provide individual and confidential mental health counseling services that are delivered away from the place of employment. If such a program is available, a staff member under stress for any reason may contact the agency delivering the service and receive help. These programs are not generally designed to deliver long-term counseling, and most employees who take advantage of this benefit use it to overcome a minor crisis. If, in the course of counseling, the problem is defined as one requiring long-term attention, then the employee's major medical benefits coverage is activated.

So often, the problems causing initial withdrawal are minor ones. The opportunity to talk about them confidentially with a trained counselor may in itself facilitate overcoming the problem. Without this service the individual may internalize the problem, and inability to discuss it with family or friends may cause the problem to grow in magnitude. This can lead to more serious mental or physical problems. In addition, it can lead to the teacher transferring the problem to the work setting and acting out his internal frustration there, rather than coping with the real problem.

Two recommendations have been made to help prevent withdrawal. First, the periodic review by the building-level administrator of staff, using the suggested questions as a basis for that review, and second, the implementation of a staff assistance program.

IN-SERVICE OF TEACHERS IN WITHDRAWAL

Periodic sessions dealing with stress reduction, building positive attitudes, physical fitness, and motivation should be a planned, regular part of the district's in-service offerings. This series should not be the same as the typical ten to fifteen session course offered for credit. Most of the people who would be interested in this type of in-service already have many credits and are not interested in taking the course for salary increments. Rather, they are interested in the topics and willing to devote an occasional hour or two to attend these sessions.

Most communities have a number of agencies that deal with mental health issues. Many of them have speakers who are available to give talks either free of charge or for a small fee. The sessions should provide techniques for stress reduction, ideas for self-improvement, and a time during which staff members can receive help without revealing their own need. If these sessions are planned in advance, advertised to the staff, and integrated into the regular meeting time, they will be well attended.

Everyone experiences stress daily, both on the job and at home. These sessions can serve a preventative function, as well as offer support to those already in the early stages of withdrawal. They could lead to a regular course dealing with stress reduction, not only for staff, but also for students. Such a course might be called, "Coping with Stress—Staff, Students, Parents."

An outgrowth of the physical fitness sessions may be groups of teachers walking together, using the weight room, or participating in aerobics classes.

All of these activities will result in staff members that are healthier, both physically and mentally.

SUPERVISION OF TEACHERS IN WITHDRAWAL

Supervision of a staff member in withdrawal should be consistent and honest. If the withdrawal is affecting the quality of the classroom instruction, it needs to be documented and brought to the attention of the teacher. This does not have to be done in a punitive fashion, since the teacher himself may not even be aware of some of the early signs of withdrawal reflected in his vocal modulation, and his motivation level.

As a routine part of the observation/evaluation process, the administrator may want to include recommended readings for the staff member. Readings should be required for the teacher in deep withdrawal, and the observations should document that these readings lead to discussions with the administrator by a specified date and then to a change in the teacher's behavior.

CURRICULUM MONITORING OF THE TEACHER IN WITHDRAWAL

Curriculum monitoring strategies by the administrator must ensure adherence to the concept of quality control. The teacher should not be permitted to deviate from the board-approved written curriculum. By the same token, the written curriculum presented to the board by the administration must be appropriate for the content area, competency of the students, and be deliverable in the amount of instructional time available. Teachers must clearly understand the goals and objectives of the content area or grade level they are assigned. The curriculum should direct instructional planning and the effectiveness of the delivery should be periodically assessed and appropriate changes should be made based on this assessment. Teachers who deviate from delivering the designed curriculum can then be held accountable.

REWARD STRUCTURE

The objective here is not to reward the negative behavior of the teacher in withdrawal. Do not overlook the late arrival or early departure. Do not ignore the failure to submit reports on time and the subtle harassment at staff meetings. Do give the teacher in withdrawal some of your informal time in an attempt to get to know him better and to determine which level of withdrawal the teacher has reached. The teacher in deep withdrawal may benefit most from your caring discussions through which he may see how leaving the system and exploring new ventures will benefit him personally. Most of the teachers in deep withdrawal are harming not only the system, but also themselves by staying in the system. Threats of removing tenure usually polarize the situation and cause other staff members to take sides. Firm, caring counseling is usually the most effective technique for encouraging the staff member to seek an alternate career.

CHANGING THE WORK ENVIRONMENT
TO REDUCE WITHDRAWAL

Reduced Workload

Changes such as reducing class sizes can be made in the structure of the school environment to help reduce the intensity and frequency of periods of withdrawal. The relationship between class size and student achievement has long been debated. Research studies have produced conflicting results. It is generally accepted that class sizes between fifteen and twenty-five students are not significantly related to changes in student achievement. Class sizes under fifteen, however, can be shown to impact on student achievement if the teacher modifies his instructional strategies to match the learning styles of the students. What about the relationship between the size and student characteristics of a class and the teacher withdrawal factor of the class? I believe that the larger the class and the greater the number of children with unique learning needs in the class, the more likely the teacher will experience negative interactions with the class, thus increasing the possibility of withdrawal. As the number of problem students increases in a class, so does the teacher's cognitive, sensory, and emotional overload. When classes are being developed, care should be taken to be sure that, when the number of problem students increases, the class size is reduced.

Availability of "Time-Out"

Everyone needs a break from his daily routine now and then. Most teachers' contracts provide for this need by giving the teacher one or two professional days to be used for any purpose. Rather than leaving the decision regarding the need for a professional day up to the teacher, administrators should be more aware of the early signs of withdrawal and provide the teacher with some alternate activities. Teachers could be assigned to visit others teaching at the same grade level or the same subject, since the limited number of in-service days provided for by most contracts restrict the time teachers have to get together across grade levels. It is not unusual for a third grade teacher in one building to not know the third grade teachers in the other buildings within the same district. Giving the teacher an opportunity to visit and observe other third grade teachers not only provides for the needed time-out, but also enables the teacher to see which techniques are being used in other classrooms to teach the same curriculum. At the end of such a day, the visiting teacher could be required to complete a short report of the visitation. Thus the teachers in the classrooms being visited receive feedback from another professional, and this kind of sharing could lead to renewal. Class visitations requiring a short report could also be arranged for other school districts. Educators frequently do this when they are considering implementing a new program, but only rarely as a preventive measure for withdrawal. Since teaching is such an isolated activity, teachers seldom get an opportunity to see their colleagues in action. It is not uncommon for high school American history being taught by two teachers in the same building using the same text to be dramatically different in content stressed, skills developed, and competency levels achieved.

Another type of "time-out" worth considering is permitting teachers with the same certification to exchange teaching assignments for a year. At the end of the year, they would return to their original assignments. Presently, teachers may apply for a transfer if there is an opening, but because the transfer is usually permanent, most teachers are reluctant to change positions. A change for one year may be much more appealing.

Balancing Stressful Work

Frequently, teachers will talk about their best class, which usually means the one with the least amount of stress, where students are on task, and there is the highest degree of engaged learning time. These are the classes in which students and teachers know they have a good chance of achieving all of the objectives for the grade or class. These are also the classes in which the success rate is high. When teachers talk about difficult classes, they are usually referring to ones in which there is much off task behavior, the students exhibit little motivation, and the classroom climate could be described as either apathetic or hostile. Difficult classes are more positively correlated to feelings of withdrawal than average or good classes. If the teaching schedule of a secondary math teacher requires him to teach three or more difficult classes exceeding twenty-five students and scheduled to be taught in the afternoon, that teacher's degree of stress dramatically increases. In some of our urban settings, these are the only kinds of classes that exist.

Nothing will increase the possibility of a teacher moving from the anticipatory stage to the withdrawal stage in one year more than putting that teacher in a stressful work environment. A dramatic example of a teacher moving from the anticipatory stage to withdrawal and then exit in five months happened in a prestigious suburban community on the east coast. The teacher had recently completed her training and finished her student teaching in the district where she was hired for a part-time position. Like most anticipatory teachers, she was filled with enthusiasm and idealism. She was assigned to teach three laboratory classes in three different classrooms. Since the rooms were the homerooms for three senior staff persons, she had to place all of the supplies she would need for a day on a cart and push it from room to room. Although the senior staff members were not rude to her, they did not make any effort to assist her or to encourage her to use the supplies or equipment in their rooms. Some kept their supplies locked away. The new teacher was assigned a desk in the science office to serve as her private planning space. The office, however, was used by many staff members, including the business manager for the high school yearbook who frequently met with students in the office before school began. Students often worked at the new teacher's desk. The teacher decided to quit in the middle of the year. The final straw came when the yearbook business adviser told her not to come into the office when the students were there. The teacher was bright, knowledgeable, and had the potential to become an expert/master teacher. If her work environment had been made less stressful, she would not have quit.

Administrators should closely review the work load of each professional to be sure that a balance exists between the number of potentially stressful classes and those which promote renewal. The teaching load and the length of a teaching day are contractually determined in most school districts. However, the composition, size, and physical space for the classes are the responsibility of the person making the master schedule. The administrator should be careful to provide a teaching schedule that reduces the possibilities of a work overload as much as possible. Research has documented the relationship between stress and feelings of withdrawal (Maslach and Pines, 1977; Pines and Kafry, 1979; Block, 1977).

School Flexibility

When teachers are involved in making decisions that directly affect them, there is less likelihood of withdrawal. This is especially true if the teacher knows that his assignment for one year, which includes three difficult classes, will be changed for the next year to include only one difficult class and he will have some voice regarding the classes to which he is assigned. Every teacher should be able to select at least one class which he wants to teach in for a given year.

Currently, most young women entering the field of teaching attempt to combine the roles of career person, wife, mother, and housewife. A full-time schedule may not always be compatible with the home situation. Districts that are willing to offer flexibility to their employees help reduce the possibility of withdrawal. Two young mothers may want to team up and agree to teach a full schedule together. There may be times in the lives of other employees when personal circumstances impinge on their ability to meet the demands of a full-time schedule. Districts that can work with their employees to develop creative solutions are districts with high teacher morale. Employees in these districts recognize that they will not be punished when circumstances beyond their control necessitate a deviation from the normal working schedule.

Opportunities for Continued Growth

Repetition leads to withdrawal, and teaching the same class for fifteen years is repetition. When a teacher reaches the expert/master teacher stage, both the organization and the teacher assume that the teacher will stay at the expert/master stage for the rest of her professional career. Wrong! Without periodic opportunities for renewal, withdrawal will take place. If the organization isn't providing the opportunities for renewal, the teacher who recognizes the early signs of withdrawal within herself will begin to question her continuation in the field.

A perfect example of this phenomenon occurred when a veteran expert/master teacher announced her resignation in the middle of the year and asked the district to release her from her contract. Discussions with the teacher revealed that upon analyzing her situation, she was certain of what the future would hold for her: fifteen more years of the same thing. She decided to start a new career in a different field. If the district had been able to provide her with a future work environment that would allow her to continue to grow personally and professionally, perhaps her decision would have been different. Some of her colleagues questioned her decision to give up the security of a tenured position to take a position in the private sector. Perhaps those who questioned her decision for that reason were already beginning the devastating trip into withdrawal.

In addition to offering in-service courses for skill expansion and development, districts should design courses dealing with techniques for recognizing and reducing stress. Many school districts employ a large cadre of school psychologists, social workers, and guidance staff. These professionals are trained to help students cope and reduce stress; teachers need the same kind of help.

Tuition reimbursement for graduate work is another way to help prevent withdrawal and promote renewal. This benefit has been eliminated from many teacher contracts due to economic constraints, yet keeping a tenured teacher in withdrawal on staff for five or ten years is far more costly than providing the financial support and incentive for teachers to continue to grow and develop. It is not unusual for a district to incur thousands of dollars in legal fees and buy-out agreements to get rid of teachers who are no longer effective teachers. The money would be far better spent by providing expert/master teachers with opportunities for renewal.

Sabbaticals are almost nonexistent in contracts today, because they are costly. The typical sabbatical will grant the teacher a portion of her salary for a year while she engages in research. By limiting the number of sabbaticals per year, the district can control the cost, but still offer this worthwhile incentive for renewal.

Work Environment

Teachers like to think of themselves as professionals. Many people agree with this, even though the unionization of the profession has hampered this professional image. Few would argue that the teachers working in our schools to transmit knowledge, socialize children, and transfer the society's values and mores from one generation to another, occupy a very important place in our culture. The work environment in which they carry out this difficult task can have great influence on their attitude and their ability to maintain a continued state of renewal. What amenities are offered in the work environment? Are teachers able to meet in a clean, cheerful, and well-lighted place that offers a degree of personal privacy when it is required? Does the staff have access to the outside world through the telephone during the course of the day or are they forced to use a public pay phone or make their calls in a public place? Are parking facilities adequate to accommodate the staff? Are there opportunities for informal social interaction? Do teachers and students have opportunities to interact informally? Teacher-student sporting events used to be common practice in schools; now they are much less common. The faculty rapport developed by a volleyball game between the male and female faculty or the male faculty and the male students builds cohesion, reduces stress, and promotes goodwill among all the participants. Acknowledging the birthday of staff members lets the employee know that someone recognized this special event and took the time to note it.

Recognition

Teacher recognition has been dealt with in several chapters of this book. It is discussed here as a remedy for preventing withdrawal. The real reward of teaching is an intrinsic one. It is that flood of good feeling that sweeps through the body of an educator when she looks into the faces of students who are trusting, anxious to learn, respectful of the teacher, and who understand the importance of schooling and feel the joy of learning. Not every class is filled with these kinds of students. Because of the student population being served, some teachers experience these rewards very infrequently.

The organization's reward structure can help all teachers remain enthusiastic. Teachers should know that the work they do is highly regarded, and that teachers and teaching are valued by the community. Churches can help by having a teacher recognition day one Sunday a year. Clubs and organizations can do the same. Businesses can place displays in their windows one week a year paying tribute to teachers. The retirement of a long-time teacher in a community can be acknowledged by the mayor or town council.

HANDLING DEEP WITHDRAWAL

When faced with the question about how many teachers are in deep withdrawal in the typical school district, the response from superintendents is usually between 3 and 8 percent. If the rate of teachers in deep withdrawal is 5 percent, most educators would shrug their shoulders and accept it as a fact of life. According to Edwin Bridges (1986, pp. 2–17) that five percent translates into over 100,000 teachers nationally who teach approximately 2,000,000 students each year. To stress this issue, Bridges estimates that 2,000,000 students exceed the combined student population of fourteen of our smallest states. Activities by school administrators to prevent deep withdrawal are not only desirable, they are essential.

The solutions offered by the numerous national reports and reform efforts focus on one or more of the following: increase teacher salaries, require competency tests as part of the admission requirements to the profession, overhaul and upgrade the quality of teacher preparation programs, develop merit pay programs, and get rid of incompetent teachers (Bridges, 1986, p. 3). The approach taken here is to be sure that the teachers hired have the highest qualifications available, and then provide a professional environment within the system to promote renewal and the continued growth of expert/master teachers by recognizing the early signs of withdrawal and intervening so that, if possible, no staff member reaches the stage of deep withdrawal.

The focus thus far in this chapter has been on the positive preventative measures administrators can take to intervene and prevent deep withdrawal. In this section we will explore more closely the teacher in deep withdrawal and suggest possible ways to deal with this problem.

While most states have included some rules dealing with removing tenure for incompetent teachers in their state codes, most of these regulations lack any operational definition of incompetence. Left to the interpretation of the administrator, incompetence is usually defined as including some deficiency in the following areas: discipline, student treatment, pedagogy, insubordination, student achievement, or subject knowledge. The determination of the extent of the deficiency and whether it places the teacher in the category of incompetence which qualifies that teacher for tenure removal is a subjective judgment largely made by the administration of the school system. This is one reason why tenure removal is so difficult.

Because of the ambiguities involved in dealing with teacher incompetence, most school districts tolerate the problem and thereby support the inept (Goode, 1967). This is particularly true if the school system is large and enjoying ample economic support. In larger, wealthy systems, incompetent teachers are often transferred around the district. The practice is referred to as "passing the trash."

Public education is often criticized for its unwillingness to deal directly with the incompetent teacher. The private sector is often used as an example of an area where incompetence is not tolerated. While the private sector does not grant tenure, they too are reluctant to deal with the emotional strain which accompanies firing an employee (Stoeberl and Schniederjans, 1981; Vogel and Delgado, 1980; Marks and Cathcat, 1974).

Tenure constitutes a property right under the Fourteenth Amendment of the United States Constitution, and as such it protects the teacher and places the burden of proof on the administration. In addition, the teacher has numerous due process rights. Among these are: the requirement of a written statement of charges and the support material to back up the charges, access to relevant documents and witnesses in the district, a hearing to review the charges, the opportunity for legal council, and the chance for appeal. The process can span a period of one to three years and cost the district from $50,000 to $150,000 (Bridges, 1986, p. 21).

Unless pressed into handling it, most districts take the route of least resistance and look the other way.

If the decision to deal with a teacher in deep withdrawal is made, the bureaucratic process starts and will continue until the case is closed, either because the teacher has resigned or the district has given up. When the process of documentation begins the administration is well aware of the fact that they are in this alone. Support from the teachers' union, the expert/master teachers in the district, the parent community, or the board is often not there publicly. The teachers' union has a legal obligation to represent every teacher in the union. Other teachers will remain quiet because criticizing another staff member is generally perceived as disloyal. Parents don't want to be personally involved although they publicly criticize the quality of the teaching staff in general. To criticize individual teachers who may be involved in legal proceedings is to invoke the possibility of legal action against themselves. School boards privately support the action of the administrators, but publicly criticize the administration if in the process not every "t" has been crossed and every "i" dotted. Unfortunately, where the actions fail, it is usually because of the "t's" and the "i's".

Once the process begins, it usually moves through two phases. The first phase is labeled salvage attempts; the second is called induced exits. Salvage attempts begin by repeatedly documenting the problems, in writing. One observation report detailing concern is not enough. Reports covering a period of one or two years that include anecdotal accounts of incidents, observations with suggestions for improvement, and documentation of how assistance was delivered and whether it was effective in remediating the problem, are essential. The documents must state specifically what the teacher's behavioral problems are and what the expected behavior is to be. Generalization will not suffice. It is necessary to document the persistence of the problems after the remedial assistance was given. A remediation plan that extends over several months is usually developed in these cases. During this period, the teacher's supervisor can expect to be accused of harassment, incompetence, and anything else the teacher can think of. Every observation will have a rebuttal attached to it, taking issue with each criticism. Other teachers who are on the fringes of deep withdrawal will come to the aid of the teacher, because they realize that if the administration is successful in dismissing the teacher, they may be next. Every teacher is effective with at least one student. The administration can expect to have parents and students come to the defense of the teacher at public board meetings. The key to dealing with this period is to meticulously document everything and to attempt to maintain emotional distance from the stresses of the situation.

Since tenure removal is so difficult, the next phase attempts to induce the teacher to leave the district voluntarily. Although the pressure applied during the period of salvage attempts is great, it is frequently not sufficient to induce the teacher to leave. More sustained, direct pressure is needed. Any and all of the following techniques may be required: gentle persuasion, candidly discussing the situation and pressing for action, increasing the amount of negative communication, using threat and intimidation, formal remediation and issuing a notice of deficiency (Bridges, 1986, pp. 77–78).

The procedures for dealing with a teacher in deep withdrawal may seem punitive, but in the end, the administrator must consider what is best for the students in the district and for the teacher's personal well-being. To continue in a role that is damaging to a teacher's physical, mental, and emotional health is not in that teacher's best interests. Although this may appear to be a hard approach given the present circumstances, in the long run the teacher may benefit in the form of improved self-esteem, productivity and long life.

Finally, if the suggestions provided in this text for dealing with teachers at the various career stages are implemented, teachers will not be permitted to get to the stage of deep withdrawal, and the actions suggested here will not be necessary.

SUMMARY

A professional who is no longer growing in his/her job is in withdrawal. Suggestions were offered to identify teachers in the initial stages of withdrawal so that they could be directed toward renewal. Although it was recognized that everyone experiences periods of withdrawal at times during his/her professional career, the depth of the withdrawal and the frequency of these periods could be minimized by learning to recognize the signs and seeking help. Finally, it was recognized that without intervention, teachers can go into deep withdrawal. A teacher in deep withdrawal is generally viewed as incompetent. Techniques for preparing the documentation to encourage the teacher to leave the district were explored.

INQUIRY

Questions and Answers About Chapter Six

Question #1: *You say that tedium and burnout often result in similar observable behaviors, how then can one differentiate between them?*

Answer: The best way to determine whether the withdrawal is caused by interaction with students or by pressures in the personal life of the teacher is to talk with him/her. Since this conversation could lead to the teacher sharing personal anxieties and painful experiences, the discussion should take place in private. If a feeling of mutual trust and support has not been created, the employee will be reluctant to share at all. In situations where the teacher is unwilling to share, the administrator will have to explore the teaching conditions and professional background of the teacher.

Question #2: *Where does a teacher cross over from persistent withdrawal to deep withdrawal? Is this difference more semantics than actual?*

Answer: Persistent withdrawal continues for a longer period of time than initial withdrawal. The teacher experiencing persistent withdrawal does not remain quiet about his/her feelings and frustrations. These teachers voice frequent negative comments. When persistent withdrawal lasts for a prolonged period of time, for example twelve to eighteen months, the chances are great that the teacher could move into deep withdrawal. The distinction among the three levels of withdrawal is more than semantic; it is related to the strength and depth of the feelings, and to the observable behavior of the teacher.

Question #3: *It doesn't appear that any one behavior would indicate the state of withdrawal a teacher may be experiencing, rather a cluster of behaviors, is that right?*

Answer: That is correct. A cluster of behaviors over an extended period of time would be needed before a determination could be made about the extent of the withdrawal.

Question #4: *Why is it that you insist on tight control between a teacher in withdrawal and curriculum monitoring? Won't this aggravate the problem further, causing even greater depression in the teacher?*

Answer: I don't think so. Anyway, the first responsibility of the system is to the student, to deliver the board-approved curriculum in a manner that will enable students to learn. Teachers must recognize that the delivery of the curriculum is not a question for debate; rather it is a requirement of continued employment in the district.

Question #5: *Some of your comments assume that the school administrator has the resources to reduce stress, particularly with so-called difficult classes. What if the options here are quite limited? Do you have any additional suggestions?*

Answer: The most influential resource any administrator has is his/her professional time. While this is not an unlimited resource, it is a powerful one. Administrators employed in districts where there is a preponderance of difficult classes, need to be sure that they are not expending all of their time handling paperwork, discipline, and resolving the latest crisis. Time must be reserved for providing the emotional support the staff needs to continue in a state of renewal.

Question #6: *You mention that all teachers are at one time or another in a withdrawal stage. What accounts for the fact that some teachers apparently go back to renewal from withdrawal without any help or assistance from the administration? Do some teachers cure themselves of this problem?*

Answer: Yes they do. In fact, that is the norm for most districts today. Many teachers recognize the changes occurring in their level of motivation regarding their profession. They see others around them who are in a state of withdrawal and they fight to avoid letting that happen to them. So they seek out ways to renew the spark, to learn new concepts, skills, or teaching strategies. In a way, they do cure themselves.

Question #7: *Other than the ones you've cited in this chapter, are there any other commonalities of teachers in deep withdrawal that you've experienced as a public school administrator?*

Answer: I'm not sure I emphasized this point strongly enough, but these teachers don't like teaching. Many of them don't like children either. They use their power over students to feed their own egos. This is the most destructive behavior for students to encounter in the school setting. If teachers in this state had an option offered to them which would result in no loss of economic benefit, they would freely leave the field. They stay because they have no other options and both they and the children suffer.

REFERENCES

BLOCK, A. M. "Combat Neurosis in Inner City Schools," Paper presented at the 130th Annual Meeting of the American Psychiatric Association (May 1977).

BRIDGES, E. *The Incompetent Teacher*. Philadelphia:The Falmer Press (1986).

GOODE, W. "The Protection of the Inept," *American Sociological Review*, 32:5–19 (February 1967).

MARKS, F. and A. Cathcat. "Discipline Within the Legal Profession: Is it Self-Regulation?" *University of Illinois Law Forum*, 193–236 (1974).

MASLOCK, C. and A. Pines. "The Burnout Syndrome in the Day Care Setting," *Child Care Quarterly*, 100–113 (Summer 1977).

PINES, A. M., E. Aronson and D. Kafry. *Burnout from Tedium to Personal Growth*. New York:The Free Press (1981).

PINES, A. M. and D. Kafry. "Occupational Tedium in a Social Service Organization," Research Report, Berkeley, California (1979).

STOEBERL, P. and M. Schniederjans. "The Ineffective Subordinate: A Management Survey," *Personnel Administrator*, 26, 72–6 (February 1981).

VOGEL, J. and R. Delgado. "To Tell the Truth: Physicians' Duty to Disclose Medical Mistakes," *UCLA Law Review*, 28: 52–94 (1980).

The exit stage.

chapter
SEVEN

Exit Stage

SOMETIMES AN END, SOMETIMES A BEGINNING

ANYONE who has been to a retirement party for a veteran teacher has experienced the gamut of feelings. Sometimes the veteran teacher is anxious to begin a new career. One teacher I know could hardly wait to open an ice cream parlor, a dream since childhood. Retirement was just a launching pad to his new adventure. In fact, he was late to his own retirement party one Friday night because he had been working at the ice cream parlor getting it ready for opening day.

Another teacher grumped all the way to the microphone to announce he wouldn't miss anybody while he was fishing for mullet in Florida. Still another wept for the old days and wished they could be relived all over again—now that everyone understood their meaning (with hindsight!).

Sometimes retirement is an end. Sometimes it is a beginning. Sometimes we don't know what it is. Whatever it is, teachers should leave their profession with dignity and respect, even if it takes some doing on the part of the board and administration to project those feelings.

PERSONALITY TYPES IN RETIREMENT

The following vignettes of retirees at parties can be related to Richard, Livson and Peterson (1968) who identified five personality types in retirement. They are:

121

—mature
—rocking chair
—armored
—angry
—self-haters

These personality types could be used as labels for stages of retirement. Looking at them from the stage perspective and then drawing relationships between the teacher career stage model and these retirement stages can provide insight into both.

Nancy accepted all of the preparation for her retirement dinner with her usual calm, composed, unruffled manner. She and her husband, Tom, had been planning for this event for the past five years. Tom had retired two years ago and wanted Nancy to retire at that time, but she wanted to wait until she had twenty-five years in the retirement system. They had purchased a lot on Hilton Head Island several years ago after an extensive search for just the right place to build their retirement home. For the past three years they spent most of their free time working out every detail of their new home. Vacations and summers were spent on Hilton Head Island in order to get to know the environment, become familiar with the shops, and get acquainted with residents in the community. They even went there during what is described as the worst season to be sure there were no surprises when the day finally came for them to move in.

About a year ago, Tom developed cancer and had to undergo chemotherapy. It was touch and go for awhile, but the cancer was arrested and now both Tom and Nancy are enjoying excellent health.

Special plans were made this year to have all of the children and grandchildren present to celebrate Christmas at the new home. The new house included a special room for Nancy and a special room for Tom. Each was designed especially for them to pursue their hobbies. Nancy had become quite accomplished at her stained glass work and Tom was into wood carving. They had begun to travel to arts and crafts fairs along the East coast to sell their creations. They planned to continue this practice after retirement.

When Nancy came up to the podium to accept her retirement gift (some specialized tools for her stained glass work) there was a slight grin on her face and a twinkle in her eye. Those who knew her well recognized these signs as ones reflecting her genuine pleasure. Nancy could be described as a mature retiree.

Mature retirees accept retirement easily. They tend to look upon it as the appropriate progression of their lives. They plan for it in advance by developing interests, friendships, and avocations which eventually will consume much of the time formerly given to the work environment. They prepared for retirement financially and psychologically. They are much more likely to focus on the positive aspects of being retired and they enjoy a longer, healthier period of retirement. The mature retiree looks back on his work years with few regrets. There is a sense of acceptance about his accomplishments and his disappointments. They don't indulge in blaming behavior. If the opportunity arises they continue to be involved in educational activities through advisory committees, volunteer work, and general support for education. These retirees find new tasks, establish new goals, and find new ways to be contributing adults. As time passes and death may take a beloved partner, it is the mature retiree who adjusts to the loss and seeks companionship with others. I suggest that the mature retirees from the teaching profession come from those teachers who were able to keep the renewal–expert/master teacher cycle going.

Phil was next to go up to the podium. Phil had worked in the system for thirty years. He was an industrial arts teacher and was always busy with special projects. If the high school play was under way, you can be sure Phil was on site working out the details of the set. Every teacher in the building knew they could call on Phil if they needed to have something special constructed for a class project. Phil had even designed and constructed the press box for the new athletic field. Phil was full of energy all day, every day!

Phil's wife died several years ago and his children lived all over the country. He had a sister who lived about twenty miles away, but basically Phil was alone. Because he was so busy with school activities, Phil had never taken the time to build friendships outside the school.

At the podium, Phil was all smiles. He had brought along a nightcap for the occasion and wore it that night. When he made his speech, he had a paper bag with him. As he spoke, he took out one item after another and symbolically threw it into the waste basket. The items included an alarm clock, a red pencil, the district's lesson plan format, and a sign-in sheet. Phil joked and laughed throughout the presentation.

The staff had all contributed to his gift, a rocking chair. This was most appropriate, for Phil was showing all the signs of a rocking chair retiree.

The rocking chair retiree views this as a time to sit back and relax. No longer is it necessary to get up at 6:00 A.M. each day and fight traffic to be at work on time. Gone are the long evenings devoted to grading papers, making tests, or talking to parents on the phone. Acting motivated, even when you didn't feel like it, is no longer a requirement. The energy level necessary to deal with twenty-five energetic second graders, or one hundred laissez-faire junior English students is gone. If the rocking chair period is a transition time for the retirees, it can be a necessary time for regrouping, setting new goals, or deciding on a new horizon to be explored. If the rocking chair time becomes prolonged however, it can lead to a negative stage. Teachers in the rocking chair stage can come from any of the career stages. If education was not the career the anticipatory teacher thought it would be and a decision is made to leave the field, a period of time may be required for reflective regrouping. This is equally true for the educator leaving the field for a second career, although these teachers tend to have planned their early retirement from the profession carefully. Because of the physical intensity required to be a classroom teacher, for almost everyone leaving the job, there is a period of time spent in this activity.

Judy knew she was going to retire in 1987 three years ago. That was when she began to join her volunteer organizations. She was president of the local Senior Citizens Club, secretary of her church circle, and co-chairperson of the Women's Club. She had asked the local teacher's association if she could stay on as president arguing that since she was retiring she would have more time to spend on the affairs of the union. They agreed since she had done a good job and since there wasn't anyone else who wanted to spend the time the position required.

Judy was planning a three-month trip to Europe right after school was out. While working as a classroom teacher she had become quite knowledgeable about cooperative learning and had led the district's in-service program. When she was teaching she was never able to accept the requests she received to speak to other teachers about how to implement a program. Now her calendar was filled with engagements.

Judy's gift was a briefcase. The teachers felt more like they were launching her into a new career than celebrating her retirement. Judy had armored herself well for her retirement.

The armored retirement stage is intriguing. People in this stage live an active, organized life to avoid the anxieties of growing old.

Although not discussed directly in the teacher career stage model, there are armored teachers in all of the career stages. The armored personality type can be positive or negative. People who have armored themselves for work or retirement do so to avoid dealing with the reality of their situation. Teachers who spend an inordinate amount of time at school are sometimes unhappy in their personal life. They choose to protect themselves from having to deal with that life, or avoid confronting their personal problems by armoring themselves with activity related to the job. The system and the community sometimes reward the individual for the long hours. The vice principal who attends every athletic event and volunteers to attend banquets, Saturday suspension, and goes on the senior trip may be an administrator who has armored himself with his job as a way of dealing with a difficult family situation. The retiree who armors him/ herself with continuous activity and who becomes labeled as a retiree workaholic is sometimes one who is gunny sacking problems. Eventually the sack will be opened and the reality of the situation will have to be faced. The armored retiree will not stay in that stage forever. Eventually he/she will emerge and become the mature retiree or the angry retiree.

Everyone braced himself for Bill. They knew what was coming. They had heard bits and pieces of it for the past year in the teachers room. Bill had told everyone that he wasn't going to come to the affair. He did come at the very last minute only because his friends had insisted. Bill's appearance was indicative of his attitude. He had on old, worn, unpressed pants, a shirt that wasn't pressed and looked as though it had been worn before, and no tie.

No one was sure what Bill's plans were after retirement. Every time a question was asked about what he intended to do, he would change the subject. He had sold his house and had not told anyone where he was going to live. There were rumors about a house at the shore, but no one knew for sure.

Unhappily, his remarks were just about what was expected. With a number of board members present and all building administrators, Bill used this time to criticize several of those in attendance. One of Bill's friends on staff finally had to get up and literally interrupt him and take the mike away from him. His friend accepted the gift, a traditional gold watch. Bill didn't stay to receive it. He left the dinner. That was several months ago. No one has heard from him since. Bill was an angry retiree.

The angry retiree is unable to accept growing old. They are people who are generally unable to accept change of any kind. In retirement they tend to talk about the good old days. Someone who was in the teacher career stage of withdrawal is a likely candidate for becoming an angry retiree. For whatever reason, they are unable to accept their circumstances. The anger doesn't help; in fact, if it goes unchecked, the retiree will slip into the next stage of self-hatred. The outward anger portrayed by these people is often a mask for feelings of inferiority. Because they question their own ability to cope, they project their anger onto others. In order to accept change, an individual must be confident in his/her own abilities. The angry retiree really doubts his/her own abilities and his/her capabilities to handle the magnitude of change required to adapt to retirement. With the right guidance, the angry retiree can become a mature retiree. Activities to facilitate this transition can begin during employment.

Ralph was too ill to come to the party. His ulcer was acting up again and anyway, if he did come he wouldn't be able to eat anything. He didn't believe in these parties. It was all a sham. The system took all of your energy, your best years, and what did you get in return— poor health, a receding hairline, and ulcers. Ralph reminded his students every day that teaching was a terrible job and he tried to dissuade them from ever considering going into the field. He was free with his sarcasm and had a reputation for failing the largest percentage of students in the science department. Whenever he was questioned about why this was the case he would reply, "Life isn't easy, I'm just toughening them up for what's ahead!"

Ralph didn't like himself very much. He saw a therapist for awhile after his wife died, but it didn't do any good. After all, it was his fault that things had gone bad for them even before Molly died. He had made some bad investments, and that second business he tried to start just didn't take off. He knew he was scmehow responsible for her depressions and he had never discussed the details of her death with anyone.

People at the party were sorry Ralph couldn't come. They remembered the days when he was full of energy. If there was a new program operating in the system, Ralph was in the middle of it, making it work. No one was quite sure when things began to change, but change they did.

Ralph was filled with self-hatred. No one knew what to get him for a gift, so they mailed a $200 money order to him. When he received it, he didn't even bother to open it for two weeks. After all, he knew anything with the school's return address was not worth opening.

Without intervention the armored retiree becomes angry and eventually withdraws to the self-hatred stage. Self-hatred is a lot like deep withdrawal. The emotions attached to this stage can literally shorten the life of the individual. Like deep withdrawal, once self-hatred has set in it is extremely difficult to bring the person back to the stage of mature retirement. Individuals at this stage blame themselves for their misfortune and sink into deep depression.

Efforts to prevent teachers from entering the stage of deep withdrawal while they are employed by the system increases the likelihood these teachers will better meet the needs of students. In addition, this activity can literally prolong the life of individuals in this destructive career stage.

IN-SERVICE FOR TEACHERS AT THE EXIT STAGE

In-service sessions for the teacher at the exit stage should deal with topics that will help them prepare for retirement so that they can enter that phase of their lives at the mature retiree stage. Districts should not wait until the announced retirement of teachers to offer this type of in-service. Districts should regularly plan a series of in-service courses designed for teachers in their forties and fifties. The great retirement lie (Lamb, 1977, p. x) says that you can wait until you are sixty to worry about retirement and that Uncle Sam will take care of you with Social Security and Medicare. Even generous retirement plans can prove to be woefully deficient if the individual lives for a long time after retirement. The inflation rate is high, and the retirement plan ceases upon the death of the retiree, leaving the surviving spouse, who has no retirement plan of his/her own, with no income.

The great retirement lie paints a picture of retirement filled with leisure to pursue hobbies, travel to exotic places, attend concerts, go to the theater, visit with grandchildren, and enjoy the fruits of the many years of hard labor. This picture simply does not represent reality for the vast majority of retirees.

In 1975 (Lamb, 1977, p. 15) the average income for persons eighteen to sixty-five years of age was $12,400. For persons over sixty-five it was $4,000. In 1971, black women who were retired had an average income of $1,000 and 75 percent of black men had an average income of $3,000. Since that time, some progress has been made, but on the whole, adults are unprepared for the devastation that can impact on their lives during retirement as a result of inflation, illness, and the shock of being unemployed.

Along with financial planning courses, the in-service program could include courses dealing with the psychological impact of retirement, starting a second business, career changes, even adult education courses that teach a new skill such as word processing or electrical repair. This type of offering shows that the district recognizes and assumes its responsibility for in-service beyond learning a new instructional technique for the classroom. These in-service sessions do not need to last for the typical fifteen hours; they can be one or two or five hour commitments. Teachers interested in this type of course do not care about receiving incremental credit on the salary schedule.

The district benefits from offering these courses by showing the employees that it cares about them beyond their formal workday and even beyond their years of employment with the district. This attitude toward exiting employees indicates to everyone working within the system that the organization cares about the human needs of its employees.

SUPERVISION OF THE TEACHER AT THE EXIT STAGE

Supervisory practices for the teacher at the exit stage can be restructured to meet the district requirements while at the same time requiring a minimum amount of time on the part of the teacher and the administrator. Perhaps the district requirement that calls for tenured teachers to be observed twice during a school year can be modified so that a teacher who has submitted a letter of resignation is observed only once. The format of the observation may be adjusted in a variety of ways depending on the district requirements. These adjustments should enable the district to meet its requirements, while at the same time streamlining the process.

This is not to say that the retiring teacher need not be observed. It does, however, apply common sense to the situation. If the teacher exiting the system has experienced some difficulty and has made a decision to leave the field for a different career, another observation which documents the deficiencies may not be required. Hopefully, the teacher's file is already complete in terms of specifying, in writing, areas which need to be improved. This strong file may have contributed to the teacher's decision to leave.

A better approach to the supervision of the existing teacher is to increase informal supervisory practices. By informally monitoring the practices of the exiting teacher, the administrator is still assured that the teacher is fulfilling his/her responsibilities for delivering the approved curriculum.

CURRICULUM MONITORING OF THE TEACHER AT THE EXIT STAGE

The exiting teacher can be invaluable in providing a smooth transition to the next teacher. No one knows a job better than the person in the job and this is especially true of a classroom teacher. Since, to a very large extent, a teacher works in isolation, he/she is in the best position to know where materials are located and how needed supplies are ordered. He/she also knows the best pacing of units, the strengths and weaknesses students tend to bring to the learning experience, the deficiencies of the curriculum and the parts of the textbook that are exceedingly good and those that are exceedingly bad.

Curriculum monitoring for the exiting teacher can include contracting with that teacher to prepare an orientation manual for the new teacher. If it is done well, this manual can provide the new teacher with invaluable guidance, helpful hints, and direction during the initial orientation period. Even if the exiting teacher is one that has been classified as staying longer than he/she should, involvement in a project such as this can be a rewarding experience for both the exiting teacher and the one who takes his/her place.

If the teacher works in an area in which a wide variety of materials is available, he/she may be engaged in preparing a detailed inventory of materials and supplies in the department or classroom. This inventory could include an annotated description of the materials and supplies, complete with present condition and projected replacement date. This type of inventory would be particularly beneficial to the new teacher in the budget development process.

The exiting teacher could be employed by the district to review all the written curriculum documents presently used in the department. Depending on the exiting teacher's expertise, this project could include updating the formal district curriculum, and could be completed after the teacher exits the system. Engaging in this sort of activity not only benefits the system, but also permits the teacher to feel the conclusion to a career which may have extended over the most productive years of his life.

In all of these activities, the administration should use discretion when making these assignments. Certainly, if a teacher lacks expertise and is perceived to be incompetent, the district would not want to enlist his/her help. However, the vast majority of teachers who retire from the system take with them a wealth of knowledge that can go unused, unrecognized, and unrewarded.

REWARD STRUCTURE

Every school district should develop a formal process for rewarding teachers who have served the district long and well. Any teacher who has worked within the system for twenty or more years deserves recognition. Quite often these teachers live within the community and their support for the school system after retirement can be quite influential in passing school budgets and referendums. At the same time, if they leave the system bitter and unappreciated, they can be just as influential in contributing to the budget's defeat.

Few systems allow their retiring teachers to leave the system without some sort of recognition. Very often, this takes the form of a resolution in their honor, a retirement dinner, or a letter of thanks from the superintendent. All of these things are worthwhile and should be continued. Some additional ways of rewarding teachers could be pursued and should be incorporated into the reward structure for exiting teachers. Each retiree could be permitted to buy $100 worth of books for the school library, or the teacher could be given $100 to buy some item for the school. Whatever the $100 is used for, the item(s) could be inscribed with the following, "Donated to _____ school in the name of _____." In a typical system of 225 teachers approximately ten teachers retire each year. After five years, the system would have fifty items with such an inscription in the district—testimony to the fact that the individuals worked in the system and that the system recognizes the contribution of its employees.

Retired employees can also be invited to serve on district advisory committees. After retirement, many past teachers like to be included in the decision-making processes of the school in some form. Serving on advisory committees is one way they can still remain attached to the system.

The suggestions offered here for in-service, curriculum monitoring, supervision, and reward structure for teachers at the exit stage are made to enhance the humane, people oriented, human development philosophy which is the foundation of this book. I believe that to a large extent, the motivational level of the employees within the system is a direct result of the administrator's attitude to the nature of the work, the role of the employee in the organization, and the responsibility of the organization beyond the formal work experience. The responsibility for promoting a positive work environment that supports and encourages both individual and system renewal, rests directly on the shoulders of the system's administrators. The institution itself has no personality apart from the personalities of the people in the organization. Therefore, the personality of the system can be directly related to that of the superintendent, the principals, the supervisors, and the board.

While this book was written from the perspective of the teacher and the teacher's career stage, the career stages model has applicability for administrators as well. If the administrators of the system tend to be in a state of withdrawal themselves, the model will not be put into effect. Only administrators at the expert/master administrator level have the personal characteristics required to implement the model. They are the risk-takers in the administration; they are the movers and shakers who can change an organization.

The exit stage of this career stages model begins when the teacher makes the decision to leave the field. You could say the teacher is motivated to leave. That motivation may occur because the teaching profession was not the right career choice for the teacher. Under the best circumstances, this realization takes place during the anticipatory stage, and the decision to leave the field is made with the cooperation and support of the administration.

Some professionals may choose to leave teaching to seek employment in another field. This can be a voluntary decision or one prompted by negative feedback from administrators supervising the teacher.

Finally, teachers may choose to leave the field to retire. Teachers at the exit stage, no matter what prompts their decision, should be permitted to exit the profession with dignity and respect.

Exiting the profession begins with the individual's motivation to change his work situation. The concept of motivation was not labeled prior to the twentieth century. In Wilson McTeer's book, *The Scope of Motivation* (1972), he traces the development of the concept of motivation from the early Greek idealists who stated "be wise and virtuous," to the opposing philosophies typified by Epicurus who professed "seek pleasure and avoid pain." He then goes on to the influences of Christianity with the opposing concepts of soul and body. McTeer continues with Descartes' substitution of mind for soul which provided psychology with its definition as "the study of the mind." Darwinian evolution followed with the shift from "What is Mind?" to "What is Mind For?" and motivation was added to psychology (McTeer, 1972, pp. 3–7).

McTeer identifies three significant developments that focused attention between 1900 and 1920 on the concept of motivation: Freud's development of and writing about psychoanalysis; Watson's concept of behaviorism; and the recognition that the theory of instinct has insignificant impact on the study of psychology (McTeer, 1972, p. 7).

The period from 1920 to 1960 saw the introduction of Kurt Lewin's Gestalt psychology, Cannon's concept of dynamic balance, Tolman's purposive behaviorism, Freud's clinical approach, Hull's publication of *Principles of Behavior*, and the implementation of many new techniques for measuring electrical charges in the cortex and mathematically analyzing their impact (McTeer, 1972, pp. 9–10). In 1972 McTeer proposed a new framework of factors which influence motivated behavior. Operating with the definition of motivation as "the active, integrated, and directed behaviors of the organism," McTeer proposed a model that includes consideration of the physical and social environment, and psychological and mental factors—all of which impact on the individual over time. Five temporal settings are identified: infancy, childhood, educational period, recent past, and anticipated future, along with the cultural geographic milieu in which the individual is socialized (McTeer, 1972, pp. 13–23).

The application of the career stages model is complicated not only because of the multifaceted nature of the design, but also because of the interactive nature of the parts. It must be remembered that integration takes place within the individual. It is within the autonomous individual that the needs of the physiological structure are combined with the physical and social environments over time, taking into consideration his/her past experiences and future goals. The model exemplifies the difficulty in understanding a human being and what motivates his/her behavior.

However, the model can be useful in attempting to understand the forces motivating a teacher to behave in a certain way. The administrator should be as aware as he/she can possibly be of the forces in each domain produced by the work environment.

For the teacher at the exit stage, future goals do not include the school setting. Depending on the teacher's age and what has prompted him/her to leave the field, the teacher could be thinking about future goals which include a new career, a retirement home, or a totally new environment. The teacher's past experiences can be just as mixed. The teacher at the exit stage may be nostalgic about the many years of dedicated service to the children of the community or he/she may be bitter and sarcastic towards the system, the administration, the community, and his/her peers.

Clearly, motivation is a multicausal force. Problems of multiple causation are not new to educators. Teachers deal with them every day in the instruction of children. Yet, we seem to persistently ignore multicausal forces in designing our staff development programs and in our day-to-day dealings with staff. We have a tendency to disregard many of the psycho-social factors impacting on behavior and to focus on one or two current environmental factors, using those to explain all of the teacher's behavior. While the multicausal approach is much more difficult, it is a more effective way to promote human development.

EXITING FOR RETIREMENT—RETIREMENT AS TRANSITION

As life expectancy continues to increase, the concept of retirement has taken on new meaning. Once thought to be the time when an individual was no longer productive, retirement today may mean pursuing a new career, entering a new life phase of which work is still an important component, or continuing in a profession as a self-employed consultant. The possibilities are limitless. These changes in attitude toward retirement have been brought about for a variety of reasons. Because of better health care, advances in medical research, sound nutritional practices, and good physical fitness, more people are living to a healthy old age in retirement. Retirement has come to mean a change in work environment, rather than its elimination.

The age at which many people seek to apply for the retirement benefits they have earned is coming down. Many retirement plans enable the worker to retire after twenty years of service and reaching the age of fifty-five. Before World War II, people generally retired only if they were forced to do so by ill health or if they were independently wealthy. The dream of being able to retire at the age of forty is less often voiced today. With a life expectancy of seventy-five years, retiring at forty would mean thirty-five years of diminished activity. This is not an appealing goal for most adults. Although the objective of being independently wealthy by the age of forty may still be a sought after goal, retiring is not.

There is an interesting parallel between the way people approach retirement and the career stages they assumed during their career: if teachers were at the expert/master teacher stage for the majority of their years in the system, they will tend to approach retirement differently than if they were in withdrawal during their years as a teacher.

Mental Motivation

A decision to exit the system after many years of service is a difficult one. Retirement brings with it the unknown. Mental factors come into play when a decision to retire is made. Freud (1935), Lewin (1936), and Tolman (1932) contributed concepts and terminology that are useful in understanding the mental side of motivation. Freud's three-compartment division of the mind into the ego, id, and super-ego, provided a framework for analyzing human behavior. The ego was given the responsibility for controlling the impulsive id and the learned regulations and restraints originating from the social milieu. Lewin stressed consciousness of the immediate present. Behavior was determined by choosing among paths leading to goals, taking into consideration positive and negative influences or valences. Tolman like Lewin placed less emphasis on the subconscious. The notion of means-ends readiness is related to Tolman's idea that behavior is motivated by the ability to attain sub-goals, which is translated to attainment of major life goals.

A decision to seek early retirement must be viewed as a means-end rather than the goal itself. Retirement in and of itself is not the goal. What retirement may bring in the mind of the retiree is the driving force behind the behavior. Unless the retirement is forced, the retiree generally believes that what is ahead will enable him/her to meet life goals better than continuing employment.

THEORIES ON AGING

A variety of theories have been used to explain the behavior of aging adults. The disengagement theory, the activity theory, and the continuity theory are three of the most popular.

The disengagement theory was first proposed in 1961 by Cummings and Henry, two American gerontologists. This theory states that disengagement, or the severing of relationships with other people and with society, is inevitable. The disengagement involves physical, psychological, and social separation (Palmore, 1981, p. 3).

Two parts of the disengagement theory have been quite controversial. First, this theory states that disengagement is inevitable. This means that no matter what the personal, financial, or physical circumstances may be, all elderly people disengage or withdraw from society and from personal relationships with friends and family. Second, that disengagement is good: good for the individual and good for society. It is good for the individual because it provides a rationale for accepting the inevitable decline of energy, and it supposedly leads to the acceptance of death. It is good for society because it allows for the transition of the roles and responsibilities of job holding and service to the community to other younger adults (Palmore, 1981, p. 4). Further, this theory suggests that because the elderly accept the inevitable, they are happier and society is not burdened with the problems associated with on-the-job illness or reduction in mental acuity.

A great deal of research has been conducted to support or refute this theory—primarily the aspect that it is inevitable, universal, and functional (Parker, 1982, p. 53). Generally, the results of this research indicate that it is not inevitable, or universal, and only partially functional (Atchley, 1972). A. M. Rose (1964), one of its foremost critics, takes the position that non-engagement seen in some elderly is the result of social-psychological factors, and is not testimony to the inevitability of disengagement. Labeling disengagement as good is a value judgement and one with which Rose takes exception. Finally, disengagement may simply be a theory with some social expediency since it seems to offer an explanation to the elderly for why they should become less involved and productive. Both Hochschild (1975) and Maddox (1968) advocate treating disengagement as a variable rather than an inevitable process, and promoting the discovery of its correlates.

Disengagement in Withdrawal and Exit Career Stages

This theory has applicability for understanding both the withdrawal and the exit career stage. When a teacher begins to feel disengaged from the system there is a sense of letting go. Teachers experiencing this phenomenon are frequently heard to say, "Let the younger staff do it. I've put in my time. It's their turn now." These people feel less desire to seek out friendly discourse during the day. It is not uncommon for them to come to work, go to their room, eat lunch alone in their room, and finish the day without ever speaking to another staff member. Administrators tend to ignore the disengaged teacher. They frequently make comments like, "Isn't it time for Joe to retire? He has outlived his time here. He needs to move along and make room for someone else." The implication is that with increasing age, disengagement from the job is inevitable. Clearly it is not a given, but it does happen to some individuals.

If disengagement characteristics begin to appear while the teacher is still on the job, without intervention, they will likely continue upon retirement. For whatever reason, there tend to be fewer disengaged teachers at the elementary level. Perhaps this is due to the tremendous amount of energy required to work with these youngsters. It takes a high-energy teacher to keep up with these high-energy students. The largest percentage of disengaged teachers appear to be working at the secondary level. A visit to the local high school early in the morning when teachers are arriving for work is a revealing experience. By watching the body posture, gait, speed of movement, and facial expression of staff members entering the building, one can almost always see a few examples of on-the-job disengagement.

Parsons (1985, pp. 49–50) takes the position that it is a crime to permit disengaged teachers to interact with students. She proposes removing these teachers from the classroom at all costs, and of course, the costs are high. She declares that "bad teachers are mean, intellectually dishonest, ill-prepared." These teachers do not like children and take some delight in their attempts to destroy the spirit of the young. Her solution is to "remove poor teachers from classrooms immediately. Let them, instead, do lunch, hall, recess, phone, and supply-room duty." She resolves, "The rotten apples must be taken out of our classrooms." Recognizing that it is almost impossible to remove tenure, Parsons would assign the grunt work of the profession to these inept teachers. Counseling for exit is another approach.

Exit Counseling

Counseling for exit is an art. The individual working with the disengaged teacher is walking a fine line between preserving the teacher's integrity and self-concept while effectuating his/her exit from the system. States which still permit buy-outs are ones where this process may move ahead more quickly and successfully. In states where retirement boards take a dim view of the buy-out practice, schools have little recourse and exit counseling is more difficult.

Exit counseling may need to start much earlier in the teacher's career. There is a national movement afoot to consolidate teacher salary guides. The assumption underlying this movement is that teachers should be paid at the top of the scale in ten to fifteen years because they have reached their maximum potential in that time. Perhaps it is time to suggest that teachers should consider a second career after they have been in the system for twenty years. Pay schedules could reflect a reduced percentage of increase starting in the fifteenth year and declining until only a cost-of-living increase is being paid after twenty years of service, unless teachers sought a re-certification degree. Teachers entering the field would do so with the understanding that teaching is somewhat like being in the military, because you could retire after twenty years of service. Of course, this would require a dramatic change in the retirement laws. However, from my vantage point, the plan has more advantages than disadvantages.

Being in the teaching profession requires a tremendous amount of energy. After twenty years of service, perhaps it is time to consider some other line of work. This is not to say that teachers of twenty-five years and thirty years should leave the field. It is not meant to suggest that the requirements for certification should be changed so that after twenty years of service there is a required re-certification process. At that time, teachers could be required to go back to school, and programs would be planned for this specialized group. Higher education institutions would be required to develop re-certification programs. After completing such a program, a teacher would be able to re-enter the field for an additional ten years of teaching. At the end of that time, another re-certification program would be required. Some states now require teachers to take additional courses to maintain their certification. However, these teachers are usually forced to select from the standard graduate offerings. Since many teachers already have their master's degree, they have to look long and hard for courses to meet their needs and interests. If higher education institutions developed a specialized re-certification program for teachers who had been in the field for fifteen years, it would better meet the teachers' renewal needs and supply districts with a continually remotivated staff.

Since the re-certification or exit option would be built into the system, little negative connotation would be attached to leaving the field. Perhaps leaving would become an expectation.

The impact on the instructional climate of the school could be dramatic. Fresh ideas would be pouring into the system at a steady rate as more staff members were replaced or reinstated after receiving a re-certification degree. The mean age of staff would be closer to the age of the students. This is not to say that older staff members cannot relate to children. However, it does suggest that maintaining the young-at-heart attitude which facilitates building rapport with students is sometimes more difficult after twenty-five years of uninterrupted service.

The activity theory (Havighurst, 1963) is in many respects the opposite of disengagement theory, just as renewal is the opposite of withdrawal. The activity theory states that disengagement is not inevitable; in fact, elderly people have a strong desire to remain involved. The activity theory requires a great deal of self-understanding. The individual must understand the personal needs and goals which were met by the work environment and find a way to meet these personal goals in retirement. These personal goals are beyond money and other material possessions. They refer to the need for affiliation, intellectual stimulation, companionship, a strong support system, social interchange, and friendship. Havighurst also maintains that the activity theory is good for the individual and for society. A supporter of the activity theory, Rhee (1974) suggests that successful aging depends on the individual's ability to continue to make a contribution to society, on his/her feelings of being integrated into society, and on his/her ability to maintain a feeling that he/she is making a contribution. Since the activity theory makes no claims to universality or inevitability, it has not been challenged in the same way that the disengagement theory has.

Szewczuk (1966) conducted an interesting study to see if elderly people who had shown definite signs of disengagement could be revitalized. His sample was composed of elderly men and women who, through a survey, had indicated that the feeling of futility was the most significant reason for their dissatisfaction with life. By encouraging these people to engage in activities such as writing an autobiography, establishing an apiary, or pursuing a new interest, a significant number of them showed definite gains in self-respect. From the study, Szewczuk concluded that disengagement was not an irreversible phenomenon of old age, that the continuation of normal activity after retirement was dependent on one's attitude that one could still be useful to society, and that engagement in a new activity facilitates the acceptance of the aging process. The activity theory has been called a theory of optimal aging (Parker, 1982, p. 60).

The parallel between the activity theory and the renewal career stage and between disengagement and the withdrawal career stage is worth noting. With both the career stages model and the aging theories, there appears to be some linkage to the internal motivation system of the individual. It should also be noted that people working or living around the teacher or the retiree may have a significant influence on his/her attitude. The message here may be that while administrators may have a significant impact on the career stages of the teacher, family and friends may have a significant impact on the attitude of the retiree.

The continuity theory (Neugarten, 1964 and Atchley, 1972) suggests that individuals may have a predisposition toward life-long experiences which is carried forward to retirement. However, whether an individual remains active or disengages is largely dependent upon a multitude of interacting biological and psychological changes, and situational opportunities. Given these often conflicting forces, continuity theory suggests that "most older people tend to maintain similar attitudes, levels of function, and activities relative to their age cohort, despite overall age changes" (Palmore, 1981, p. 4).

The same statement could be made for the career stages model. Most teachers tend to maintain similar attitudes, levels of function, and degree of competence relative to their years of experience, despite overall life experiences. Perhaps some teachers are destined for withdrawal from the time they enter the field as anticipatory teachers. If administrators are doing their job, these teachers will be identified during the non-tenured period and will not be granted tenure.

SUMMARY

By exploring the personality traits of retirees and theories of retirement, this chapter examined the relationship between personality characteristics, retirement theories and the career stages model. Relationships between the personality characteristics of the mature retiree and the expert/master teacher were noted, as were the relationships between the teacher in withdrawal and disengagement retirement theory. It was noted that one's approach to life is far more related to behavior and attitude, than whether the individual is categorized as employed or retired.

In addition, suggestions for monitoring the professional behavior of the exiting teacher were made. Since this is a time of transition, it is a time to relax the formal administrative practices commonly attached to the observation/evaluation process.

By promoting feelings of positive self-worth in the exiting teacher, the individual leaves the system with a sense of accomplishment and fulfillment. By assisting the exiting retiring teacher in avoiding disengagement and promoting mature retirement, everyone gains: the system, the administration, and most of all the exiting teacher.

INQUIRY

Questions and Answers About Chapter Seven

Question #1: *What have been the most effective cooperative endeavors for retirement efforts you've seen?*

Answer: The most effective retirement effort I have seen is one which was jointly planned by the association and the board. The date was announced early in the year and everyone looked forward to the occasion as a celebration of the end of the year and a time to stop and reflect about each attendee's accomplishments. It was a dinner-dance and spouses and friends were encouraged to attend. The music was danceable and the banter was light and humorous. It was a time for gental roasting of the staff, the administration, and the board, in addition to honoring retirees. While the retirements were an important part of the event, they were only a part of this happening. Everyone was invited: secretaries, maintenance staff, aides, teachers, administrators, and board members. Retired teachers were also encouraged to attend. The evening not only brought closure to the year, but also was a time for noting the major accomplishments of the system. Everyone left the event with a sense of achievement and looked forward to the next year. Stuck away in the back of their minds were thoughts of next year and the comradery to take place again. These events became the benchmarks of accomplishment for the system. They provided for healing and renewal at the same time. Everyone started the next year with a clean slate.

Question #2: *Do you think all teachers should have some basic psychological counseling, no matter under what conditions or with which feelings they may be leaving the district?*

Answer: To recommend some basic psychological counseling for each staff member who is about to retire is not necessary. What is necessary is to be sure that any staff member, retiree or not, who is experiencing difficulty coping with any of life's stresses, feels comfortable seeking temporary assistance from a counselor. When extended families used to live together, there was almost always someone who became designated as the family member to whom one could go to talk things out. As the living arrangement of families changed, counseling became less often a function filled by a family member and more often one filled by a trained counselor. Since counseling is becoming more accepted, it carries with it less of a negative connotation. This change should help retirees and non-retirees.

Question #3: *How can retirement be made a celebrative experience?*

Answer: Retirement should be a celebrative experience. It should represent the culmination of a rich and full work experience and represent a reward for long years of effort. It can become just that, if the individual facing retirement, plans to provide the necessary economic support for the period of retirement far in advance. The individual will also need to prepare him/herself psychologically to deal with the loss of the work experience. Some people fail to develop an identity apart from their work. These are the people most vulnerable to the negative impact of retirement.

Question #4: *What parallels do you see between the cycles of retirement and the career stages model?*

Answer: As pointed out in several places in this chapter, I see quite a lot of parallels between the cycles of retirement and the career stages model. I think this is particularly true when comparing the mature retirees with the expert/renewal teacher. Both are well-adjusted, in control, and thoughtfully guiding their lives. Likewise, the activity theory of retirement parallels to a certain extent the renewal efforts of teachers. At the same time, I see a relationship between the angry, self-hater retirees and teachers in withdrawal. I also see a relationship between disengagement theory and withdrawal. The angry self-hater retiree blames himself and his environment for whatever negative circumstances he finds himself in.

REFERENCES

ATCHLEY, R. C. *The Social Forces in Later Life.* Belmont, California: Wadsworth (1972).

CUMMINGS, E. M. and W. Henry. *Growing Old.* New York:Basic Books (1961).

FREUD, S. *New Introductory Lectures in Psychoanalysis.* New York:Norton (1935).

HAVIGHURST, R. "Successful Aging," In *Processes of Aging*, R. Williams, C. Tibbits and W. Donahue, eds. New York:Atherton Press (1963).

HOCHSCHILD, A. R. "Disengagement Theory: A Critique and Proposal," *American Sociological Review*, 10 (1975).

LAMB, T. *The Retirement Threat.* Los Angeles, California:J. P. Tarcher, Inc. (1977).

LEWIN, K. *Principles of Topological Psychology.* New York:McGraw-Hill (1936).

MADDOX, G. L. "Retirement as a Social Event." In *Middle Age and Aging*, B. L. Neugarten, ed. Chicago:Chicago University Press (1968).

McTEER, W. *The Scope of Motivation.* Monterey, California:Brooks/Cole Publishing Company (1972).

NEUGARTEN, B. *Personality in Middle and Later Life.* New York:Atherton Press (1964).

PALMORE, E. *Social Patterns in Normal Aging: Findings from the Duke Longitudinal Study.* Durham, North Carolina:Duke University Press (1981).

PARKER, S. *Work and Retirement.* London:George Allen and Unwin Ltd. (1982).

PARSONS, C. *Seeds: Some Good Ways to Improve Our Schools.* Santa Barbara, California:Woodbridge Press (1985).

RICHARD, S., F. Livson and P. G. Peterson. "Adjustment to Retirement." In *Middle Age and Aging*, B. L. Neugarten, ed. Chicago:Chicago University Press (1968).

RHEE, H. A. *Human Aging and Retirement.* Geneva:International Social Security Administration (1974).

ROSE, A. M. "A Current Theoretical Issue in Social Gerontology," *Gerontologist,* 4 (1964).

SZEWCZUK, W. "Rehabilitation of the Aged by Means of New Forms of Activity," *Gerontologist,* 6 (1966).

TOLMAN, E. C. *Purposive Behavior in Animals and Men.* New York:Century (1932).

Administration: career stages model—implications.

chapter
EIGHT

Using the Career Stages Model: Implications

LEARNING IS THE BOTTOM LINE

IT ought to be clear that the career stages model for classroom teachers is not based upon bureaucratic or budgetary constraints. As opposed to external requirements in schools, the career stages model is centered on the internal state of being and the competence of teachers.

Likewise the career stages model is not focused on the age of the classroom teacher as some new models appear to be. An age-based approach to differentiating among teachers is unnecessarily deterministic. There is nothing one can do about one's age. Furthermore, an age-based model of classroom teaching doesn't account for the fact that there are very mature teachers out there who are still young at heart, keenly effective, energetic, and competent.

Any model that doesn't take into account a person's state of mind and motivation to use one's professional skills over time, is bound to be irrelevant to children and to what they learn. Fancy career ladders will ultimately crumble, not because they can't be implemented or because teachers may like or dislike them, but because they don't make a difference in what children learn in schools. And as far as public support is concerned, learning is the bottom line!

So this chapter is concerned with how to think about putting a career stages model into practice and some of the barriers one can expect to discover in the process at the federal, state, and local levels.

IMPLICATIONS FOR THE FEDERAL LEVEL

For the past eight years of the Reagan administration the efforts in regard to teachers have been largely unproductive, antagonistic, and superficial. The President has personally pushed merit pay as an antidote to the problems his administration perceives with teachers.

His administrative officials have taken a tact that actually reinforces most of the negative and debilitative conditions already at work in the schools. External manipulation of salary is perhaps the least effective and least promising strategy to improve the overall strength of the teaching cadre, because it has little to do with the internal forces that actually motivate that cadre (Herzberg, 1966). The hidden assumption of this administration is that there has to be some way to "get the turkeys" in the teaching cadre, as if the teaching cadre were filled with such creatures, and there is no way to change them except by weeding them out.

Furthermore, tuition tax credits and voucher plans have no promise to change the status quo. As a "fear factor," they are based on the assumption that because of a lack of competition, teachers now are not doing their best. If the base of public support were placed in jeopardy, this fear factor would motivate them to higher levels of productivity.

Frankly, there is already too much fear in schools. Too many school districts face financial uncertainties that lock them into a siege mentality precluding any serious or deep-seated change from actually occurring. When a human organization is dominated by a survival mentality, it has little incentive to introduce radical alternatives (Hasenfeld, 1983, p. 244).

Also, the assumption is often unstated that there must be some new and improved technology out there that teachers are failing to employ because they lack the motivation to use it. All that is needed is to force them or scare them into applying it and the schools will automatically be better. There is no evidence that such an educational nirvana exists anywhere. There are no mysterious technologies that are kept in some secret hiding place or are opposed by the majority of the current teaching cadre. The evidence indicates that what is known about teaching and what makes it good is part common sense and part research-verified common practice. We know of no teaching model or system that wasn't used in some way in the schools prior to being sanctified by research. So what is missing? And how will any strategy fill that gap?

What has been observed is that too many politicians want solutions without knowing what the problems really are. For example, merit pay is a solution, but what is the problem? Too often the problem is that the pet solution isn't being applied. That forces one into a kind of elliptical solution application modality rather than a problem-solving modality. An elliptical solution application modality is, "We need merit pay. We don't have merit pay. That is the problem. The solution is to apply merit pay." The so-called need is the preselected solution. It is a self-fulfilling prophecy applied, in which case, the evaluation consists of whether or not the prophecy was applied, and not what problem was solved. The problem is always erased by the solution because they are one and the same.

Politicians want to get re-elected, so they have to solve problems within their term of office. That ensures that long-standing, deeply ingrained and complex problems are glossed over with quick fixes so that they can be traced to a direct, public benefactor. There are few significant problems in education that this author knows of that can be solved in any elected official's one or two terms in public office, whether at the federal, state, or local level. A politician who always demands that problems be solved in his/her term of office perpetuates the worst kind of educational faddism and misuses of public funds. It means that federal and state officials are constantly dragging out from the past the most absurdly simple solutions to longstanding, hard-rock problems. And as successive administrations come and go, their reforms are like the waves splashing on the rocks at the shoreline. They may make pretty pictures for seashore artists, but the substance is hardly changed over time.

What is required is a strategic planning approach rather than a tactical Band-Aid approach. The planning horizon, to be realistic, must span one or two decades. And the strategic planning mode should be a patient, deliberate process that is rooted in gaining a workable consensus about the problems among all of those involved, and not just quick fixes. And most of all, we must avoid the gong of doom cacophony of nations at risk or last chance for our children (Honig, 1987) strains that perpetuate our problems rather than leading to real solutions. Whatever problems schools may have, they didn't get that way overnight, and they won't be solved overnight.

Despite the wailing of some of the "reformers," public education isn't about to collapse. The stock market may crash, but the schools will not. They may slide, but the movement is very slow. Virtually every major candidate in the 1988 presidential election made public statements about education. So, while their planks may be global and vague, the fact that they view education as important is at least affirmed. With that as a positive leaning, the federal effort would pave the way for improvement by facilitating solutions applied at the state and local levels.

The career stages concept is not a solution. Rather it is advanced as a condition, a given of the teaching cadre. The description of the career stages model in this book might be incomplete or even erroneous when it comes to the precise nature of the differentiation levels among teachers, but the fact that there is such differentiation now, and that it should be paramount in approaching solutions, is believed to be correct.

The federal effort would be grounded in affirming both those factors that lead to the enhanced competence of the entire teaching cadre rather than merely a piece of it, and those programs and actions which will produce renewal within the largest part of that cadre.

Creation of a National Academy of Teaching

The National Academy of Teaching would not be the same as a national examination board for teachers. That approach is for licensure. The National Academy of Teaching might perform the following functions:

(1) Perform and gather case studies of great teachers, creating a significant data base grounded in outstanding practice

(2) Offer scholarships to classroom teachers for sabbaticals to improve their knowledge of the subject matter and its transmission to classroom practice, thus reducing the lag time involved in the current textbook development and adoption process, or within collegiate pre-service programs

(3) Promote the creation and development of alternative schooling environments that are based on the learner rather than being dominated by the bureaucracy (McNeil, February 1988, pp. 432–438)

(4) Foster a spirit of what Giroux (1983) has called a hermeneutic rationality. "Meaning in this mode of rationality is not removed from the worlds of the social actors who constitute, shape, and live within its definitions." Hermeneutic rationality would focus on how teachers within schools can negotiate and re-negotiate the social reality they confront on a day-to-day basis. It is the centerpiece of a truly reflective teaching practice. This thrust of the National Academy of Teaching would not seek to merely perpetuate a repetitive teaching practice, but expand and challenge that practice through a rigorous internal examination of teaching and schooling as it is commonly understood.

This last dimension requires a caveat. The National Academy of Teaching is not a "think tank" dominated by college professors more interested in reading papers at scholarly conferences than impacting practice in real schools. It is an action-oriented agency that is promoting a rigorous reflective teaching practice. It is neither all theory nor all practice. It is a living example of the connection between the two. In the past, colleges of education strove to fulfill this function, but they failed to do so for reasons which will be explored later.

(5) Hold regional conferences to promote critical thinking and oustanding practices. Each year the National Academy would hold four or five regional conferences in which the best national and regional practices would be highlighted. To some extent, associational activities now do this. However, too many associative/union conferences focus on such topics as collective negotiations, fringe benefit issues, conflicts with other administrative groups or school boards, or the political action agenda of the organization itself.

While these are important areas of concern, they are more related to associational activities per se than forming the nucleus of a concerted thrust to improve teaching practices in the schools. The National Academy would be free from having to expound or include these topics. Nor would it be an end-run around the matter of teacher unionism. Legitimate teacher concerns, as expressed through their own associations/unions on matters for which they could bargain would not be the subject of emphasis at the National Academy. Neither the necessity for unions, nor the work of the United States Department of Education would be supplanted. That agency primarily carries out the laws enacted by Congress. As a federal agent, each department's major officers are political appointees who have, in the past, exhibited distinctively skewed agenda towards educational issues. This problem is not expected to change.

The National Academy of Teaching would function as a separately funded agency, whose professional appointments would be secured by a National Board of Classroom Teachers and Scholars chosen by a bipartisan committee of Congress for uneven, rotating terms. The leadership roles of the National Academy would be for ten year periods to ensure consistency of approach and continuity of effort. Funding would be guaranteed not to fall below a minimal level stipulated by law. This guaranteed fiscal floor would ensure that short-term projects, which may be controversial in nature, are not aborted before they can be explored fully and completely.

In short, every effort would be made to protect the National Academy of Teaching from undue, partisan political influence, to secure independence from associational/union agendas and from the Department of Education's political appointees, and to shield it from being vulnerable to sudden shifts in public popularity. By doing so, it would also be able to resist being thrust into a search for Band-Aid remedies to deep-seated problems in the schools. Its staff would have the protection to speak out vigorously on the issues of the day. The National Academy's ten year planning horizon would provide the leverage to espouse the long view rather than the short. For such an agency to fully engage in a reflective practice, these kinds of minimal guarantees would at least ensure that it has a chance of being realized.

Creation of a National Thrust to Promote a Movement Dealing with Teacher Shortages

Periodically the nation has faced teacher shortages and oversupply. There is no central planning function to guide states, colleges, and universities from doing anything but following a kind of boom and bust cycle of marketplace mechanics. The problem is more complicated than that. Because education is a state function, the individual states pursue their own ideas of what constitutes adequate teacher preparation apart from every other state.

So let us say that state X in one region of the country passes a law requiring a certain score on the NTE (National Teachers Exam) and a fifth year of preparation. The legislature wants to improve the quality of teachers serving in the schools of that state. Yet state Y produces a surplus of math and chemistry teachers (almost no state prepares enough physics teachers) but only requires a four year baccalaureate. Instead of state X being able to attract state Y's teachers, two barriers have been erected to prevent the shortages in one area from being filled by another area's surplus. For experienced teachers, the chief drawback of moving across state lines is leaving a state's retirement system. Some teachers face substantial losses of income in their senior citizen years for having moved out of their state's retirement system.

State by state, this system forces the continual recurrence of a very costly duplication of effort. The individual states must always face enormous sunken costs to start up a program and maintain it, rather than simply being able to adjust to the larger marketplace dynamics. And it also means that those states with more limited programs must strive to duplicate expensive programs of larger, more wealthy states, while at the same time keeping training programs in states with an obvious oversupply of teachers (such as in male physical education) from closing down their programs. Programs must be maintained for fear of the costs of having to start up again once the supply has met the demand.

Imagine trying to run the U.S. Army on the same basis as education is run in the nation. Each state would have to have its own infantry training program, tanks, intelligence, artillery, and air force. Suppose state A trains a large supply of artillery personnel but state B doesn't. State B can't shut down because it would have to start up its program at some point in the future, but it doesn't know when. Thus, the nation would suffer from having unbalanced military preparedness because of the peculiarities of state by state training. Artillery training might be superior in one area, but dismal in another. The ability to improve the overall level of effectiveness and efficiency would be hampered by outmoded regionalism and barriers that impede the movement of personnel from an area of oversupply to an area of shortage. From a national viewpoint, the resources expended by the states do not add up to any maximization of their impact *as a nation* and prevent the states from optimizing their investment because of disproportionate wealth and population distribution trends. In short, the taxpayers get no breaks by being able to capitalize upon economics of scale beyond the state level and are caught up in funding diseconomies.

Short of a national teaching certificate which would mean creating some sort of national agenda and agency to perform this function, there ought to be better coordination among the states to capitalize upon trained personnel in the country, and to facilitate their movement from state to state. That would mean easing the penalties involved for teachers in terms of their retirement benefits should they desire to leave one state to pursue teaching in another. Such a national system exists at the collegiate level in the form of TIAA-CREF and covers professors in both public and private institutions. This greatly facilitates professorial movement, which in turn is an enhancement for career renewal.

The states now have large numbers of their teachers as virtual captives, good or bad, motivated or disenchanted, energetic or cynical, within their borders. Change is a vital ingredient in maintaining renewal. When all possibility of change is closed out, there are few incentives via movement within teaching to stimulate growth. It is a detrimental condition to not only the teachers, but to students and taxpayers as well. It is the perpetuation of a system in which most everyone is a loser at all levels of educational governance: local, state, and federal.

The federal government is in the best position to carry out this coordination, because it is involved with the movement of personnel across state lines. It can assume the responsibility for funding some of the inequities which will arise from doing a better job of coordinating supply and demand in the collegiate preparation of the nation's teachers. Compensation might occur in several forms. First, the government might offset losses of income to teachers in the retirement system of a receiving state. Thus, if a teacher from New York were to move to Mississippi, he or she could not expect the same level of retirement, and/or a loss of some years from one retirement system to the other. The federal government might offset that loss by reimbursing Mississippi, which would in turn continue the same benefits for the teacher after the move to Mississippi as he/she could have expected in New York.

Second, the government could offer grants to teachers in the form of free loans or scholarships to offset any increased preparation costs by teachers who moved from one state with one set of certification standards to another requiring stiffer standards. The matter is achievable if there is a will to make it happen. It is believed that maintaining teacher renewal by promoting improved teacher mobility across the nation accomplishes two things simultaneously. First, it creates strong incentives for staying on the cutting edge professionally, and second, it enables the nation as a whole to reduce its investment in costly duplication of training which perpetuates its problems with funding education, state by state, or as a nation.

STATE ISSUES AND PROBLEMS

Within the respective states, there are a number of barriers to successfully taking advantage of the career stages concept. The first suggestion will not be popular on the surface with state affiliates of teacher associations/unions.

Change the Probationary Period to Obtain Tenure

Most tenure laws assume that every teacher should automatically obtain tenure after three years. This goes directly against the fact that not every teacher grows at the same rate, or that individual growth rates can somehow be absorbed within a three year period. This is patent nonsense.

Some teachers might be ready for tenure after one year of service, and others not until five, seven, or perhaps ten. Tenure laws were passed for a reason. History has shown that teachers were dismissed because of their sex, religion, political persuasion, marital status, or popularity. If there were no real reasons for tenure, it would not be a reality today. There is little to suggest that conditions have changed so that competent teachers do not require protection for the same reasons. Even in America toward the end of the twentieth century, without tenure, Socrates might still have to take his cup of hemlock.

Yet the three-year tenure period for every teacher is absurd. The non-tenure period ought to be expanded to seven years for local school districts. Certain provisions could be included in the policy to ensure that some unscrupulous school boards or administrators do not use this circumstance to avoid making a decision, or to keep down dissent within the ranks.

For example, the administration would have to make a hard case before a state arbitration panel, which would issue a ruling on the matter of any teacher not recommended for tenure at the end of the three-year period. If it were deemed that there were sufficient data to support the administration's decision, the probationary period could be extended. If not, the administration would have to make a recommendation on that teacher to the Board of Education as it would have done under the old three year or "out" law.

I would disagree with association/union types who argue that three years is sufficient time for a teacher to obtain tenure. The reality in schools is that most administrators function with a span of control that far exceeds what is generally accepted to be effective. Management literature generally agrees that, for effective supervision, six to not more than twelve teachers should be monitored by any one administrator (Mintzberg, 1979, p. 134). There are few schools in which this span is a reality. Many principals function with spans exceeding thirty teachers and some go on up to more than one hundred.

Now couple this fact with the actual time available among a principal's many duties to be able to directly observe a teacher (see Finch 1981, p. 338). What I am talking about is the "sample" which the principal or other administrator must use to decide upon the tenure matter.

The typical secondary teacher is instructing approximately five periods a day for about one hundred and eighty days per year. That comes to nine hundred periods of instruction. Under most teacher association/union contracts, an administrator is required to observe a teacher for about three full periods of instruction. Three periods is less than one percent of the total time that teacher has been teaching! In this case one percent of a sample of a typical secondary teacher would constitute nine full periods of observation. Given the excessive span of control of most school administrators, to observe a classroom teacher for one percent of the total time he/she is with children is almost an impossibility, not to mention the possibility of being charged with harassment!

While it's true that some administrators don't know very much about teacher observation or don't offer practical suggestions to improve teaching, more often than not it is true that, even if the administrator was competent enough, he/she simply doesn't have the time to do it.

I know of several cases where an administrator recommended not providing tenure because of sufficient doubt in his/her mind that the teacher would or could improve. Given the relative permanency of what tenure means legally and practically in most school districts, administrators cannot give teachers the benefit of the doubt, because they face the possibility of living forever with a mistake if one is made. Thus it is much safer to dismiss a teacher if one has doubts, rather than put one's hope in the "goodness of humanity." If the administrator had the option of lengthening the probationary period to provide more time, more teachers might eventually gain tenure and be better teachers for it as well. This procedure would conform more to the reality of individual human growth and to the reality of how schools are commonly administrated. The creation of an impartial and binding third-party panel would be a sufficient deterrence against local abuse, particularly if that panel were composed of at least half classroom teachers who were considered expert/master teachers from across the state.

Re-Define the Nature of Staff Development

School districts ought to be required to develop a comprehensive staff development plan based on a solid assessment of the career stages and skills of their teachers. That, in turn, should qualify a district for state financial support to engage in meaningful and relevant staff development. This means that the idea of staff development becomes more than asking the local college professor–who may not be a very good teacher him/herself–to come in and "talk to" the staff for an hour of two about motivation. One-shot staff development has given the concept a bad name with most teachers. They view it as another "dog and pony show" they must endure to satisfy the administration or the legislature that they are "up to speed." Under such circumstances, staff development is a costly joke, because by adding all the salaries of the teachers who were not instructing children for a day, it becomes clear that this is one of the best prohibitive/expensive activities the district could undertake. For example, from a small school district of one hundred teachers who make an average of $20,000 for a 180 day school year, the cost per day would run about $11,000.00, or about the salary of a part-time teacher for the year. If two full days per school year were devoted to staff development, the cost would be equivalent to the salary of one additional classroom teacher. Because of the way staff development is conceptualized and implemented in most school districts, hiring additional staff and reducing class size accordingly would be a far better investment.

On the other hand, differentiated staff development by career stages can provide teachers with the focus and the stimulus to engage in personal change, improve specific professional skills, experience continuing professional and personal renewal, and serve as a stimulant to maintain the energy of the staff in the process. That kind of staff development strikes at the core of what motivates people: achievement, growth, and recognition. It is worth every penny.

Define a Minimum Level of Expectation

Unfortunately, many local school boards are dominated by interests antithetical to what is good for children or teachers. In some cases, boards and the administrators who work for them have become corrupt–catering to the lowest level of greed, nepotism, and profiteering. There aren't many, but in various states such districts are well known as educational cesspools.

Philosophers might argue that such excesses of the democratic process are inevitable, but will work themselves out in time. How long will such places be allowed to continue to shortchange children? How many lives will be damaged because of a faulty education? How long will the scars last?

Lately, several states have introduced the equivalent of "educational bankruptcy" bills (Pipho, February 17, 1988, p. 27). These measures are designed to set up criteria by which the state will intervene and clean up the corruption that has prevented a school district from providing a quality education to its children.

There is evidence that the possibility of a state takeover must become real in order for some districts to take steps to rid themselves of the corruption that occasionally produces a headline or ends up on national television (Hasenfeld, 1983, p. 244).

The states must take the lead in dealing with corruption that is deeply embedded in local mores. Otherwise children will be denied an education guaranteed by most state constitutions as their rightful inheritance.

No approach to teachers will work if a school district's condition has shrunk to levels which sap its will to improve, and infects its personnel with the same disease. The states must establish the mechanism to right the local education ship of state when it cannot right itself.

Provide Competent Technical Assistance

Many state agencies have neither the personnel to regulate effectively, nor the staff to assist local school districts in improving their operations. Each state agency must take steps to seriously examine whether its personnel is strong enough to work under difficult conditions, and competent enough to make a difference in improving school operations.

The reputation of some state departments of education in the country is almost bankrupt itself. State department people are seen as political hacks, cronies of the politicians in power, who trade in money and influence instead of an earned respect based on the ability to solve real problems in real schools under the actual working conditions of teachers and administrators.

Involve Expert/Master Teachers and Other High-Quality Local Leaders

State leaders must take steps to involve local expert/master teachers and outstanding local administrators in state efforts to improve locally operated educational systems. Such local expertise will help refine state efforts and provide additional state credibility in dealing with the more difficult local school systems. In some states it is too easy to take pot shots at those bureaucrats in the state capital. It is less easy when they are joined by competent and caring local personnel with an established reputation for excellence.

Establish Statewide Teaching Academies

Many states have established summer principal academies. Few have moved to the next level to provide intensive summer experiences for outstanding teachers. Such teachers could be nominated by their respective associations and/or school boards or superintendents, and could be the subject of improved visibility for their excellence in the classroom. They could be given enlarged district responsibilities for supervision. They could also provide specific types of in-service for their own staffs after a summer experience.

Academies that "pass muster" with local school folk have to be good. They must be action-centered and practical, enabling teachers to transfer ideas, concepts, and skills from one situation to their own home environment. As such they must usually be taught by colleague practitioners instead of college professors, unless the professors have been exceptionally good practitioners and can model what they preach. The problem with many professors is that they can't do what they expect their students to do in the work setting in which their students must function. Credibility in any mentoring or coaching relationship is based on the understanding that one's mentor or coach can in fact do what you are trying to do. College professors often come up short.

Improve the Data Flow to Colleges/Universities to More Effectively Adjust Preparation to Supply/Demand Requirements

Ask a college dean if the state regularly provides him or her with data about its anticipated teacher vacancies of the next ten years, by subject field. The states that provide such information to their preparatory institutions are rare indeed. Many colleges and universities have no idea what the state-wide demand for teachers in specific disciplines will be within even the short time frame of two to three years, let alone longer range data.

State departments of education should improve their personnel forecasting capabilities. Such data would help in statewide efforts to recruit teachers from out of state, to provide various types of incentives to colleges and universities to recruit more students in areas expected to be in short supply, and to accurately inform college students about employment if they insist on going into an area of teaching that is already glutted with qualified candidates.

Form Partnerships with Business and Industry

Many large school districts have initiated efforts to involve the business community in the schools. Some state departments have taken the lead here as well, but it is still not common enough. Business and industry could provide summer scholarships to expert/master teachers for renewal experiences, fund travel or international teacher exchanges, or even lend personnel to the schools to be short-term teacher trainers. The biggest danger of linking up with business and industry is that business leaders too often have no real in-depth knowledge of school operations, assuming that glitzy solutions in their world are quickly transferable to education. Business leaders may often be too hasty in grasping at quick "fix-its" instead of helping the schools to come to grips with longer range, more difficult problems that require sustained support. Unless business or industry wants to end up permanently supporting the schools, they must offer the kind of help that is ultimately transferrable to the hard money budget and is translated into firm general commitment from the public at large. Philanthropy will only take a public service so far in improving its quality over a sustained period of time. Many business leaders have no real appreciation for the politics of education. They should be reminded that if they were to run their businesses like schools, they would have to hold a general stockholders' meeting every Monday night, and from this meeting translate the decisions made there into company operations on a weekly basis.

IMPLICATIONS FOR THE LOCAL LEVEL

The local level was once where the action was in education. Now, in many areas, the major initiative has shifted to the state level. Yet there are still many things the local school board and chief school officer can do at the local level to promote improved instruction based on the career stages idea.

Initiate Efforts to Spur Local Teacher Renewal

Once it is understood that teachers in renewal require support, visibility, and recognition, boards can take steps to discover who their teachers are, highlight them in staff newsletters, and articles in the local press and recognize them at back-to-school night.

Boards can also fund substitute teachers to enable staff to attend state and national conferences in their areas of interest. Travel and participation at state and national conferences is a strong motivator for professionals. While all but a few school districts have abolished the idea of sabbaticals, the few that still use them have a potent tool for personal and professional renewal.

Of course, if the board perceives such activities to be too costly, of dubious value, or visualizes them as "junkets" instead of serious work-related activities, this avenue of renewal will be lost. Then too, a Board may not be cognizant that they have to invest in people to maintain their currency. Teachers can get stale, and since few of them can be fired, it makes good sense to make them the best possible.

But many school board members have a myopic view of these activities that lead to renewal. They should be reminded that over 70 percent of their budget is in people. The schools are no better than the teachers, administrators, secretaries, custodians and other persons in them. Seventy percent is the major investment of a school system. Looked at one way, staff development based on career stages is a strategy to ensure that the taxpayer's investment is maintained. It's the same argument that good schools keep up the property values of the homes in the community, i.e., one has to spend some money on the most precious asset any school system possesses to make sure its value is maintained.

In small systems, board members sometimes get too involved in personalities. They may think of Rosey Jones, that sloppy fourth grade teacher, who is sometimes rude to parents and is personally unattractive and lazy. The idea of Rosey going to a state convention is simply too much for some to take. What do they think will change Rosey? They've tried everything else, including fear, and she's still there.

One of the major players at the local level is the school superintendent. The superintendent has to be convinced that investment in people makes sense, and that it is one of the few options open to the school system to improve the quality of its services where they count the most: in the classroom.

A question that usually comes up relates to the effectiveness of well-known, but expensive in-service speakers. Most superintendents and boards wince at the price of bringing in a Madeline Hunter with a $2,000 to $3,000 price tag for one speech (Stover, January, 1988, p. 17). Yet is it really all that expensive? Assume for the moment that the district could get Madeline Hunter for $2,000 plus expenses. Assume the expenses run $1,000 including airfare, hotel, meals. If the district had 100 teachers, the cost would be $30.00 per teacher. Compare these figures with those resulting from sending all 100 teachers to a state or national convention to hear Madeline Hunter.

What does the district receive with a big name speaker? Such speakers are usually guaranteed to be good. They wouldn't command that kind of money unless they are good. So your staff will be exposed to the best. They will be listening to a world-renowned professional. That is something upon which future activities can be built. A Madeline Hunter type speaker is worth what they charge, as long as the district capitalizes on the event for future development. As a one-shot occurrence, as good as Madeline Hunter may be, nothing much is gained if the district doesn't use the occasion to launch a solid follow-up program (Stallings, 1979, p. 174).

Now compare that decision with one where the district brings in the local professor from State U. You may be lucky and end up with a budding Will Rogers, or a waiting-to-be-discovered Madeline Hunter. Chances are you won't. If they are that good, they will be known already. Listen to the tales of veteran superintendents who have discovered that a cheap speaker who bores his or her teachers or, worse yet, insults them with corny stories or theoretical claptrap, learns that not only will the staff never consider that topic again, but they will also wonder about the intelligence of the administration who brought this "turkey" in to talk to them.

Veterans on the speaking circuit will tell you almost universally that classroom teachers are the most difficult, the most cynical, the most negative, and the rudest audiences they face. Some would walk a country mile to avoid them. Others double or triple their fees when the audience will be exclusively teachers.

The reason is not hard to discern. Every day classroom teachers face the most difficult audience of all: our children. These kids are amused nightly by a billion dollar entertainment industry that has used every sitcom gag our grandfathers might still not have heard after years of attending vaudeville.

Teachers know what it is to be under pressure to perform with this generation. They live with those pressures every day. Good teachers are performers (Lessinger and Gillis, 1976). So if the administrator brings in a professor or anyone else to teach teachers, they had better be good at their craft. It would be like a group of actors going to see fellow actors perform. What non-specialists would miss, teachers never miss. If a superintendent has laid out $11,000 for a large group session and then employes a $150.00 speaker who blows the whole thing, the $11,000 has been blown, too.

However, one also has to be realistic about what can be accomplished in a fifty or sixty minute speech, no matter how good it may be. About all that can be done is to provoke awareness, raise consciousness, introduce some basic ideas, and hope it is well done and motivational to boot. In-depth understanding, deep-seated change, and serious and sustained personal introspection are rarely, if ever, the result of a one-hour lecture, no matter who is giving it.

For the most part, local efforts to engage the staff in renewal activities must depend on a different strategy. That strategy is the equivalent of taking the district's expert/master teachers and using them to plan and execute days in which the staff must examine their own skills and potency in the classroom, behind closed doors.

Some of the most successful, truly renewing in-service activities happen when teachers structure their own time for other teachers with help and support from the board. For true solidarity to occur, for a communion among colleagues, teachers must share a sustained experience with one another over several days. They must be able to work and play together, be comfortable enough to let their hair down, and laugh at their own foibles and faux pas in school. That kind of staff development does happen, but is quite rare. Too many administrators are uncomfortable with their own teachers and can't let their hair down in front of them. Consequently, not only do they never know them, but they never create the cohesion it takes to engage in the type of renewal that can move human mountains.

For personal examples of this kind of intensive experience I will cite two districts. The first is Janesville, Wisconsin. Every year for the past four years, Superintendent Donald Mrdjenovich has taken twenty to thirty teachers to a weekly retreat. They live, eat, and sleep in one facility, share their meals, work, and party together. The first year, Mrdjenovich got the Parker Pen Foundation to sponsor the retreat. After that, because of its success with teachers, the board of education included it as a budget item every year. The teachers who have attended become alumni, and will reunite one evening at the Yahara Center in Madison, for a time to renew what they experienced together that week in mid-August. Mrdjenovich brings in speakers from all over the nation. They are among the best that can be found. The teachers have an opportunity to break bread with them, and speak face-to-face informally about areas in which they share a deep concern for the future of education.

The second experience is the annual retreat of the staff, secretaries, librarians, administrators, and teachers of the Walworth Barbour American International School in Israel. The superintendent, Forrest Broman, takes the entire staff on a weekend retreat to the Sea of Galilee. There, amidst the shadows of an ancient crusader fortress, Mount Ida, and the Golan Heights, the staff works all day and launches into the evenings with a hilarious teacher talent show that spoofs the administration, educational trends, and international developments and dances; they play Trivial Pursuit and engage in other teacher designed contests.

The retreat speakers are a combination of local staff (an Israeli novelist, a political analyst), some educational experts from the U.S., and plenty of expert/master teacher talent. That talent leads the seminars, takes other teachers on archaeological walking tours, and engages in aerobics and folk dancing. The atmosphere is relaxed but intensive. The sessions are a mixture of humor and seriousness, frivolity and depth. Teachers talk about the retreat all year long. It is the event!

These two examples are rare. I don't know of too many other places where the type of communal *esprit de corps* is built along these lines. Contrary to what some might think, teachers, like other human beings, covet meaningful interaction. They appreciate candor; they enjoy all kinds of humor because they experience it as a matter of course in their work; and they respect competence because they have the responsibility for developing it in young people.

Because teachers are performers, they appreciate a good performance. And they appreciate not performing a "plain Jane" speaker who tells the unvarnished truth. Such events as I've described create a kind of "bonding" effect in a staff for which almost no other experience can serve as a substitute, except perhaps a crisis like a strike. Yet, much of a strike is negative and damaging to interpersonal relations, leaving scars that run deeply for years after it happens. Strikes are a poor way to foster esprit.

Creating a critical mass of teachers who engage in renewal requires an event that a significant number of the staff experience together. Retreats are an excellent method to accomplish that. But they have to be well-designed and planned, or they are likely to turn into nothing more than an all-night party. Real bonding occurs with work and play mixed together. The play is necessary to help reduce tension and let off steam when a staff is seriously engaged in reflection and thought. Devising the right combination to produce maximum results takes experience and good planning.

Differentiate Staff Development Based on Career Stages

It isn't so much that staff development has been totally ineffective in most school systems; it is, rather, that it has been effective with too few teachers. The ones that were in renewal stayed renewed. The ones that were not in renewal, usually the majority, weren't renewed. Renewal is more than inspiring talk or an occasional uplifting message. Renewal occurs when a teacher relates his or her own personal growth to that of the system, or put another way, when a teacher's energy towards improvement also improves the instructional program of the school and the school district.

One-shot staff development sessions simply don't do enough for most teachers. They aren't powerful enough to engage the mind and muscles of the larger teaching cadre to put forth the effort to begin the hard process of thinking seriously about purpose, examining content and pedagogical skills, and setting forth in a new direction with some confidence.

A more productive way of thinking about local staff development is to differentiate among staff and try to be "on target" with more teachers by recognizing that not all require the same thing. Teachers in renewal should receive some attention to stay renewed, and there should be a lot of teacher input into the planning and execution of staff development. In addition, these members of the professional staff should have more autonomy than teachers who are still in the anticipatory stage. Teachers in the exit stage should receive an even different type of treatment.

Our thinking ought to become more "clinical," not in the sense of being antiseptic, but in the sense that the treatment should fit the dilemma, and not the other way around. Local educators have to look at their teachers as being different because they are different.

Be There When Good Teaching Happens

It may sound corny or trite, but administrators, particularly superintendents, simply aren't in the school buildings enough. If an activity is honored and held in great esteem, it also gets the most attention of the "powers that be." A lot of good teaching goes unnoticed and unsung. Much data for this consists simply of listening to a lot of colleague superintendents talk about what they do and what they are concerned about. It isn't that they aren't concerned about good teaching; heaven knows they complain enough about the lack of it. The fact is that they don't think it is important enough to get out of their offices and go to observe it, praise it, make it visible, and elevate it.

The superintendent can issue all of the memoranda he or she wishes about the importance of good teaching, but there is no more effective barometer of good teaching's importance than being in the buildings when it happens, even becoming part of it on occasion.

If one is in the buildings enough on any kind of regular basis, one hears about special teaching events, a culmination unit, a creative project, or a new technique. One can also get invited to come see. Since teachers work alone, it is important for them to have people that make a difference appreciate what they do. Parent and student appreciation is important, but the support and understanding of the boss is crucial. Remember, there aren't any raises in schools based on performance that amount to much, if anything at all. Verbal praise, or a thoughtful review of something that is going on, is all a teacher is seeking.

The reader is asked to recall—if he or she was a classroom teacher—how many times in the course of a day one wished one's boss had been there to witness the first time Harold, a student with problems, "caught on" and became part of the class; or Suzy, the girl who could never do long division, finally mastered the steps; or a creative class designed a one-act play. So many of those little events pass without fanfare and without honor, that many teachers wonder what in the world the administration is talking about in improving teaching. They don't even know what is going on now. How would they know if it were improved in the future? So teachers toil on, finally coming to the conclusion that those people at the upper echelons are really more concerned with other matters than what the teachers do. They are, after all, just teachers. In the end, the message we give teachers is by our actions, not by our words. When administrators are there when good teaching happens, it is sanctified and recognized in its own house where it counts the best. A banner from the U.S. Department of Education might fly on the flagpole, but the most important and motivating factor for teachers is the personal human touch of the people they count on to understand what they do, day in and day out. No banner can be a substitute for that.

Avoid the Application of Negative Satisfiers

Like any working cadre, teachers normally complain about things. It isn't their complaining that is necessarily a problem, rather it is *what* they are complaining about. Most work groups complain about working conditions, and there are plenty in teaching that are demeaning and nasty.

Most teachers eat in less than fifteen minutes, though their contracts might specify a longer period of time. Teachers learn to work under continual pressure from maintaining the work flow of students in a variety of activities, and to do so without having to go to the restroom for longer periods of time than most adults find normal.

When teachers aren't surrounded by children, working with an individual child, sitting in conferences about children, talking on the telephone about children, or meeting parents about children, they have to watch children eat in cafeterias, play on the playground, board buses, pass in the hallways, use the toilets, shower and dress, and observe them engage in some physical intimacies in the hallways, cars, parking lots, or anywhere else students may be inclined to engage in such activities. In addition, they must supervise children at games, dances, plays, debates, clubs, or performances of various kinds. Unlike most other professions where the professional has some "down-time" to think and be away from the pressures of responding to clients all the time, teachers have no such span. They are surrounded by a relentless work routine that completely submerges them for long periods of time without rest or repose.

This work environment puts human beings constantly on the edge. Teaching is an activity that totally engages the adult. Teaching is 100 percent active duty. That is why teachers are so sensitive about morale. When one's energy and patience are wearing thin, one notices the little things more distinctly. Little annoyances can become big ones overnight. So some outsiders think teachers are overly reactive and defensive about criticism. That observation is undoubtedly true in some cases. Yet, rarely does there seem to be much appreciation for why teachers are that way. Normal, rested, healthy adults can bounce back from reasonable ups and downs of the job. Yet a comparison to normal jobs would reveal that teachers work under constant pressure. They are like educational air traffic controllers in schools. The unyielding intensity of the work environment is especially demanding on the physical and mental resiliency of the people doing the work.

It is because of this climate that teachers are so resentful of cries for more paperwork of any kind, especially since they can't do paperwork in their offices since they have no offices to go to. They have no personal secretaries to type the paperwork or to make phone calls for them. In short, teachers have no support staff, something even the lowest middle management non-professional working in any other environment has access to. Paperwork means one of two things. It either means subtracting personal time from children, or taking it home. Both are odious choices.

Much of the so-called accountability legislation has increased teacher and administrative paperwork. Principals' desks are overflowing with it. Who usually has to complete it? Teachers! These are negative satisfiers; they subtract from the energy of the teaching cadre. They build resentment, hostility, cynicism, and indifference. What has happened to teachers has also happened to physicians. If you have been to your doctor's office lately, have you noticed how many extra staff members are around to process the Medicare and health benefit forms? The same load has hit teachers, but there is no support staff to pick up the burden.

At the local level, administrators should take steps to reduce paperwork. That can take the form of combining information required on one form, adding to the secretarial staff, purchasing computers to pick up the clerical slack, and beginning an educational campaign to inform school patrons of how the work environment has changed in schools. Of particular importance is the local school board's understanding of negative satisfiers. Every request by the school board for more information must ultimately be translated into some kind of paper trail. Too many boards are insensitive to the fact that every interesting question they might think of must somehow be answered by a human being or lots of human beings supply-

ing the information. Some board members bombard their administrators with demands for information they will never use in decision
making, but which they want to know because a parent asked for it,
or they might use it someday, or they want to satisfy their own
curiosity about something. More than once, when teachers com-
plained to boards about too much paperwork, the board turned to the
administrators as the culprits, although the administration was
only trying to answer the board's own quirk for information.

FUNDING STAFF DEVELOPMENT AT A HIGHER LEVEL: PROTECTING A PERISHABLE ASSET

There is no good cheap staff development effort. Human time is
normally the most expensive kind of time around. One-shot deals,
quick fixes, and cheap but good programs to improve teaching are
not only unproductive, but sometimes destructive of their own stated
goals or intentions. In the end, boards will simply have to pay more
to get more, and they must get more than they have been getting.
The teaching cadre is the most expensive and most important asset
any school district possesses. It is an irony that in some districts, the
board spends more money on preventive maintenance of its school
buildings than it does on staff or human development of its teachers.
Funds for the renewal of the teaching cadre are like preventive
maintenance. They work against the trend for human capital to
become stale and unproductive. Human capital represents 70 percent or more of the total district resources year in and year out. Investment in teachers is necessary to protect, maintain, and enhance
the most important but most highly perishable assets in our schools:
the morale, vigor, competence, and motivation of its teachers.

COLLEGES OF EDUCATION

Colleges of education should have been the places where renewal
was built into the process of training teachers. Unfortunately, as an
overall generalization, that has not happened.

One of the ironies in this dilemma is that too often good teaching
is not recognized, honored, or rewarded in the one place where it
ought to serve as a beacon of brilliance: in the college of education.
The reason is not too hard to explain. Colleges and universities have
been completely captured by the quest of research, and only one kind
of research. Research, not teaching, is the most prized activity at the

level of higher education. Research wins grants. Grants lead to funding the university's overhead, paying for graduate assistants, and maybe Nobel prizes. Where does teaching fit in? Nowhere.

Then, too, the salaries that education professors earn are considerably below those of many experienced elementary and secondary school teachers. So who wants to be a college professor in education? The answer is: someone who couldn't make it in a regular elementary or secondary school, who is more interested in research than teaching, and more interested in producing scholarly papers than in preparing able practitioners for the schools. In many ways, universities themselves are at fault for the dismal reputations of their colleges of education. There are some really good colleges of education that do a sound job in preparing classroom teachers. They aren't necessarily the ones that are ranked periodically in higher education circles based on the number of papers read at research conclaves. Rather, they are the ones, despite the absurd pressure to conduct research, where able professors prepare able teachers. Unfortunately, there are too few of them, and they also go unsung, and may even be criticized for their lack of scholarly output.

There have been all kinds of national reports aimed at correcting the situation. One of the most cited was the Carnegie Forum's Task Force on Teaching as a Profession *A Nation Prepared: Teachers for the 21st Century* (1986). The Carnegie Forum was comprised of teacher union leaders, members from the business community, a dean, several commissioners of education, and other dignitaries. A critical omission was the absence of any school administrator or school board member. This was unfortunate since the implementation of the Forum's recommendations would have a pronounced impact on the school principalship and other administrative roles, and local costs would increase.

Among the recommendations of the Forum were:

- a National Board for Professional Teaching Standards
- the restructuring of schools to provide a professional environment for teachers
- restructuring the teaching cadre, introducing the role of Lead Teacher
- requiring a bachelor's degree in the arts and sciences as the entry to teaching at the undergraduate level
- develop a Master of Teaching degree in graduate schools of education

—increase the number of minority teachers

—relate student performance to incentives for teachers

—make teachers' salaries competitive with other professions

Many of the recommendations of the Carnegie Forum are also supported by the rationale underlying this book. Yet others are naive and possibly misdirected.

For example, it is highly doubtful that a National Board of Professional Teaching Standards would add much to what is envisioned as the improvement of professional practice. In the first place, the issuance of certificates that had any weight would require significant agreement among all fifty licensing agencies in the U.S. That would mean abandoning the idiosyncracies of the respective states. It would mean that a teacher who is issued a national license by the central board may not also have to pass the Arizona Constitution test for the license to be valid in Arizona. Similar peculiarities exist in a number of states. In addition, having a national certificate would force some states to adopt the standards of others, mostly premised on the assumption that more is better.

While the Carnegie Forum attempts to separate certification from licensure, indicating that the National Board would certify, and the respective individual states would license, the real result would be a two-tier system of paper credentials that must be secured by a prospective teacher. That simply adds to the problem of getting qualified people into the profession. It is unlikely that this effort will drive up standards in some states because that would substantially increase the costs of teacher preparation. In times of scarcity, state legislatures have a habit of lowering standards by inventing channels to allow more people into teaching. When times get tough, the bottom license will always prevail, and it is more market sensitive than anything else.

A National Board of Teaching Standards has long been an agenda item of teacher unions, who believe that it is a strategy to bypass the control of entry now existing at the state level, and a place where union presence can be maximized. In many states, the state agency doesn't really certify, rather the colleges of education recommend to the states who is eligible to be issued a state license.

The National Board of Standards is an attempt to centralize teacher licensing in the United States. Under one light it could be *the channel* to foster improved teacher mobility within the nation, if only one license were required. However, under a more realistic light, it will add another bureaucratic layer to an already cumbersome process of becoming a teacher. In the end, the states will prevail. There is no evidence to suggest that the respective fifty state legislatures are in any mood to agree on a universal set of standards that would mean entry to their state based on national certification. They are much more likely to agree on a two-tier system. That would simply add to the problem.

The second Carnegie recommendation that is also echoed by the Holmes Group (1986) pertains to undergraduate teacher education. The Carnegie Forum takes aim at the fact that undergraduate education majors should be a thing of the past. They point out that some teachers can't spell, write, or compute well. The solution is to have prospective teachers enrolled in the arts and sciences and be the beneficiaries of a liberal education. This would "deepen appreciation of our history and culture, foster an understanding of the theory and application of science and technology, develop aesthetic sensibilities, and inspire creative impulses."

There are several fallacies in this Carnegie Forum recommendation. How many second grade teachers have failed as teachers because they couldn't explain or read a passage by Chaucer, Blake, or Milton? How many teachers were ever dismissed because they couldn't explain the basic assumptions of causal relationships in pre-Newtonian science? Ask any school administrator who has ever fired one. They will say that teachers are usually fired because they couldn't teach, couldn't create order in the classroom, or ran amuck on any number of organizational-ethical issues. The greatest number of failures as teachers is because teachers can't teach. That centers on pedagogy, the real issue, right where it belongs.

If teachers are not literate with the language or nominally competent in arithmetic, is placing them in arts and sciences the answer? How many colleges of arts and sciences are geared to teaching or want to teach basic skills that exist in a pre-collegiate curriculum? A liberal education goes far beyond the mastery of these elements, and it isn't a guarantee that teachers will be able to spell or compute either. There are plenty of physicians who can't spell or write legibly, corporation executives who depend on their secretaries to correct their spelling, and Presidents of nations who depend on corps of speech writers and other media wizards to perform their jobs. Few of these people were education majors.

That doesn't detract from the ideal that all citizens ought to be literate, that they ought to be able to use the language reasonably well, and ought to be able to function within our society and survive and contribute to its growth and change. Basic skills are a prerequisite for participation in a liberal arts curriculum, not its principal reason to exist. A liberal arts curriculum ought to open one's mind, but there are plenty that don't. The difference is in the way they are taught. It is a matter of pedagogy.

Dropping the undergraduate education major and funneling all those students into arts and sciences will ensure that prospective teachers will take more credits in the arts and sciences than before, but it won't ensure that they will be better teachers than before. That is still a matter of pedagogy. And it won't help in deflecting the current criticism of teacher education that exists now. In fact, it will ensure that criticism is more focused than ever before because the only responsibility colleges of education will have is the fifth year. The excuse of the undergraduate education major can no longer be used. My prediction is that teachers will still fail because they can't teach, and colleges of education will still be blamed for it. And the colleges will respond that instead of the fifth year, they will require a sixth or seventh year, because one simply can't learn all of pedagogy in a year. The knowledge base will have expanded, research will have proceeded, and what other profession has only one year of pure professional preparation? This recommendation of the Carnegie Forum is misdirected and will only succeed in delaying a solution to the problem.

The real solution was touched upon by Harvard's Derek Bok who indicated that colleges of education had failed to do the only thing that they were really set up to do: to build a reputation based upon their special competence in education (*The International Educator*, 1987, p. 1). By agreeing to end the undergraduate education major, colleges of education have simply abrogated that responsibility, admitted they haven't done it, and cast serious doubts on their ability to deliver any better instruction in a fifth year. In short, the problem has been pushed around, but not solved!

One of the promising recommendations of the Carnegie Forum is changing the school structure to create a more professional environment. That means introducing less of a custodial baby-sitter model in schools, using staff more flexibly than before, and instituting a diversity of professional and paraprofessional roles that are now largely non-existent.

The most serious obstacles confronting this proposed change are the lock-box classroom structure that exists in schools and the assembly line scheduling models that dominate their operations. These models are pervasive and deeply embedded in custom, practice, and law. They will not easily be cast aside and will invariably lead to additional costs, which may not always be translated into an immediate gain by students on a standardized test. Thus, some educators and citizens looking for the "quick fix" will not find this recommendation simple or attractive. Yet in the long run, it has a lot of potential for salutary change.

What Can Colleges of Education Do?

One way to improve the teaching of pedagogy is to change the context in which pedagogy has traditionally been taught. Pedagogy has been taught in college classrooms. It should be taught in context in real schools, similar to teaching hospitals. The Holmes Report (1986) has called such sites Professional Development Schools (p. 56). Here college professors serve on staff as resources and adjuncts to the schools. At such sites, college professors do demonstration teaching, conduct on-site research with teachers as colleagues, and engage in scholarly inquiry to examine teaching *in context* under the actual conditions that exist in the schools.

These requirements would move the faculty of colleges of education to place more emphasis on the actual teaching skills and abilities of their professors, and elevate teaching to greater prominence. Professors ought to be assigned at least one semester every two years to teach and conduct research in an operational school.

Governmental agencies ought to refuse to fund educational research that is not directly connected to teaching hospitals or professional development schools. That would ensure that research is conducted under actual conditions of practice and is always connected to practice. A lot of the research would result in greater benefits to teaching instead of supporting graduate students who simply go on to study teaching. Another requirement that would be beneficial is for those universities who are not engaged in teacher preparation in any significant way, not to be as eligible to receive research funds to improve teaching as those who have large enrollments in their colleges of education. The money ought to go to the sites where large numbers of teachers are being prepared. In some cases, those state universities that have large teacher preparation programs have not been receiving significant funding to improve teaching. Funding has often gone to a few prestigious "think tank" institutions whose faculty is more interested in publishing scholarly papers and books than improving practice in applied settings. Funds ought to be going to where the bulk of teachers are being prepared, in order to maximize the impact of improving the eduation of teachers overall. In the long run, that strategy would pay off in both quality and quantity of improved teacher preparation for the largest percentage of the nation's teachers. That strategy would also help shift the resources of educational research to applied settings and reinforce the importance of teaching on those campuses where colleges of education have not had access to the kind of or level of funding that colleges of medicine or engineering have enjoyed. In short, the money is spent where the real action is.

Finally, it ought to be noticed that if colleges of education did not exist, they would have to be re-invented all over again. Nowhere on most university campuses is teaching qua teaching studied. Some brilliant college professors, renowned scholars of worldwide repute, are abysmal teachers and survive only because they bring prestige to the university and/or are good at grantsmanship. Their students learn because they can rise above the poor quality of instruction and are sufficiently motivated to do so. Place that renowned professor in a public high school with a class of non-voluntary, non-motivated antagonistic young people, and he or she would be eaten alive for lunch.

There are some things we know about pedagogy. A study about teaching has not been totally barren or completely unproductive all these years. Some arts and sciences professors could profit enormously from a short course with Madeline Hunter, and their teaching would be substantially improved. Teaching is more than telling. It is a complex, dynamic, mutually interactive, and contextually grounded endeavor. It is a living interchange between generic and idiosyncratic forces, not the least of which is the personality of the teacher mixed in with the panoply of student-related variables.

Where are these relationships studied? Where is the most fundamental process of social reproduction analyzed? Where does one engage in a study of teaching to be a teacher? In colleges of education. We have them because teaching as an activity in society is of such compelling importance to ensure its enhancement and survival.

Schools of theology exist to prepare ministers, schools of law for barristers, schools of medicine for physicians, and military academies for admirals and generals. Teachers and administrators are prepared in a college of education. Wherever this specialization in society, the equivalent would also exist as a formal institution. The location of this "place" on a university campus offers some protection from teachers becoming the trained police agents of the state or being enlisted in overt political acts of pure indoctrination. Within the confines of the tenets of academic freedom that exist on most university campuses, teachers can be prepared in an environment that protects and honors the search for the truth, no matter how unpopular that search might be.

Were teacher preparation to be removed from the university setting, one has to wonder where it would be located and what social and governmental pressures would be exerted upon that "place" in the licensing of the nation's pedagogues. A de-centralized approach is the best guarantee of the preservation of the basic freedoms most Americans still enjoy. The first act of repression of the young must begin with the enslavement of the teaching cadre by the state. Certification from the university or college setting is a great bulwark against any temptation to intimidate the nation's future by any acts of political hegemony. Before it is changed, the consequences ought to be seriously contemplated.

SUMMARY

Capitalizing upon the practical application of the career stages concept means thinking about ways to use what is already reasonably well established regarding ideas of human motivation. Humans are seen as purposive creatures, moving in one direction or another. They are not inanimate objects simply responding to stimuli (McTeer, 1972, p. 12).

Changes in the social environment can trigger varying responses, depending on where people thought they were going, and can actually effect possible changes in career patterns. By so doing, as social changes alter future possibilities, human direction and motivation take into account a different array of options. Human perception of different futures can alter human responses in the present. Whether humans are moving toward or away from such futures depends upon their attractiveness or anxiety in the mind-set of those viewing them.

There are major efforts currently under way to change the conditions of teaching, the role of the teacher, and the means by which teachers have been prepared. Some of the proposals look promising; others appear to be very unrealistic about attaining the professed change. Still others are actually regressive upon close examination.

The least promising of all is the idea of bureaucratic ladders based on seniority and budgetary requirements which ignore the actual growth stages of teachers in their daily work. This proposed change will be explored in greater detail in the next chapter.

INQUIRY

Questions and Answers About Chapter Eight

Question #1: *Why haven't models of careers for teachers used the idea of teacher stages if it seems like such common sense?*

Answer: One of the political problems in the public sector is dealing with certainty. One must have objective criteria in order to stand up under scrutiny. Look at the frantic search for tests in assessing teachers in states that have implemented career ladders. Age and seniority are also objective in the sense that they too can be easily established. While many are aware of the varying motivational levels of teachers, the matter of certainty is far less stable, thus ensuring that even if a paper and pencil measure could be shown to be valid, there could be a problem with reliability. That means that if a state were challenged legally to prove that a teacher was at one stage instead of another, it would be difficult to find data that are not a matter of opinion and judgment. This raises the issue of favoritism which might be hard to rebuff. For this reason, I see the career stages model as a focal point for staff/human development and teacher preparation and not as an approach to salary determination in the schools.

Question #2: *You seem to have some reservation about a National Board of Teaching Standards as embodied in the Carnegie Forum, but have no trouble embracing a National Teacher's Academy. What's the difference?*

Answer: The difference lies in the purpose of the two agencies. A National Board of Teaching Standards is aimed at accomplishing uniformity among the states in teacher certification. A National Academy of Teaching is aimed at cataloging great teaching, stimulating discussion that is divergent, even heretical, about teaching as a technical and political act. Were the National Academy of Teaching to foster uniformity among certification, I would also be opposed to it.

Question #3: *Wouldn't the creation of a system to promote teacher mobility actually create a national system of teacher certification, something which you oppose?*

Answer: It may in fact happen that way. However, the control remains firmly in the hands of the states and not in an agency at the federal level, whether governmental or not.

Question #4: *What is the biggest problem in moving towards your recommendation of extending the probationary period for teachers?*

Answer: Well, of course, some state teachers associations may have a quick "knee jerk" reaction, believing that this is just another proposal to attack tenure. I'm not opposed to tenure for teachers. History has demonstrated rather amply that tenure has protected teachers for all the right reasons, but it has protected the marginally competent or even mediocre teachers as well. I am proposing an extended probationary period to ensure that when tenure is offered, it is based on a firmer data base than exists now in many school systems. I fully recognize the danger for administrative abuse, and I would not advocate extending the probationary period without very tight due process and review procedures built into it. I think that if pursued within these guidelines, there may be less abuse, an incentive for strengthening the quality of teacher evaluation by school administrators, and fewer cases of unjust dismissal. The current period is simply not adequate for all teachers, and works against one who got off to a bad start. I have had personal experience in this regard. The current legal framework offers no compromise about this recurring personnel problem.

Question #5: *Isn't the example of the weekend retreat for staff a bit unrealistic? If it isn't, why is it not common practice?*

Answer: One reason for this is that the idea of one-shot staff development is still the major delivery mode in the minds of boards, legislatures, and too many administrators. It is based on the assumption that the teaching cadre is an undifferentiated blob that needs "it," whatever the latter might be. That model ignores the internal mind-set of teachers to direct their own work within the confines they establish, which is exactly why it has not been a very effective tool to promote change in the schools.

Another factor is the we-they polarity that exists between administrators, teacher union leaders, and some teachers. To a certain extent, administrators and union leaders have a vested interest in promoting conflict because it justifies the need for their roles. A retreat implies that combatants learn how to approach one another in a problem-solving modality, as opposed to an adversarial one. It takes great maturity and diplomacy to shift gears. Conflict is much easier. The most vulnerable people however, are the adminstrators. Unfortunately, many of them believe the old adage that familiarity breeds contempt. If they believe it, they are probably right. After all, they know themselves better than anyone else.

Question #6: *Why is it that so many teachers are critical of their courses in colleges of education?*

Answer: I think the answer has two parts. First, too many of their professors did not model what they preached. Teachers who teach teachers ought to be superb models of teaching themselves. Secondly, the teaching of methods courses was done out of context. When teachers got into the actual work context, they couldn't transfer what they learned to the immediate challenges they faced on a day-to-day basis. The classroom context is like being in a shooting gallery with multiple stimuli all at once.

The typical college classroom is indeed a serene place, where concentration on one or two variables is possible. But that is never the real world of classroom teaching. I have argued, and it is not original with me as I pointed out in this chapter, for contextually based teacher education, such as teaching hospitals in education.

REFERENCES

Carnegie Forum on Education and the Economy. *A Nation Prepared: Teachers for the 21st Century* (May 21, 1986). Excerpts appeared in *The Chronical of Higher Education*, p. 43–54.

FINCH, M. "Behind the Teacher's Desk: The Teacher, the Administrator, and the Problem of Change." *Curriculum Inquiry*, 321–342 (1981).

GIROUX, H. *Theory and Resistance in Education.* Massachusetts:Bergin and Garvey Publishers, Inc. (1983).

"Harvard President Raps Ed Schools," *The International Educator*, 2, p. 1 (October, 1987).

HASENFELD, Y. *Human Service Organizations.* Englewood Cliffs, New Jersey: Prentice Hall (1983).

HERZBERG, F. *Work and the Nature of Man.* New York:World (1966).

HONIG, B. *Last Chance for Our Children.* Reading, Massachusetts:Addison-Wesley Publishing Company, Inc. (1987)

LESSINGER, L. and D. Gillis. *Teaching as a Performing Art.* Dallas, Texas: Crescendo Publications, Inc. (1976).

MINTZBERG, H. *The Structuring of Organizations.* Englewood Cliffs, New Jersey:Prentice Hall, Inc. (1979).

McNEIL, L. "Contradictions of Control, Part 2: Teachers, Students, and Curriculum." *Phi Delta Kappan*, 69, pp. 432–438 (February, 1988).

McTEER, W. *The Scope of Motivation.* Monterey, California:Brooks/Cole Publishing Company (1972).

PIPHO, C. "Academic Bankruptcy—An Accountability Tool?" *Education Week*, 7, p. 27 (February 17, 1988).

STALLINGS, J. "Follow Through: A Model for In-service Teacher Training." *Curriculum Inquiry*, 163–181 (Summer, 1979).

STOVER, D. "In-service Hotshots: Are They Worth It?" *The Executive Educator*, 10, pp. 15–18,29 (January, 1988).

Tomorrow's Teachers. A Report of the Holmes Group. East Lansing, Michigan (1986).

chapter
NINE

Leadership and the Professionalization of Teachers

CHANGE IN THE CURRENT STRUCTURE OF SCHOOLS

TEACHER and teacher scholars invariably look toward medicine, law, and theology when the subject of professionalization is mentioned. Teachers want to be like doctors, lawyers, or ministers. They want autonomy from boards of education and administrators; they want to set their own rules about what to do; and they want greater control over who can become a teacher. What they often forget is that these other professions have developed some other hallmarks that teachers don't have or aren't particularly keen about acquiring. What teaching has not yet developed is an esoteric knowledge base (see Olson, March 2, 1988, p. 7). Such a base would discourage a talented layperson from attempting to be a teacher. For example, a layperson would be reluctant to perform complicated surgery without training. Likewise, one would not want to represent someone in a messy trial without the proper legal training. Without some formal theological preparation, it would be difficult to preach from some pulpits; though with some Christian fundamentalist sects, untrained amateurs have been known to rise to prominence.

It is still possible for persons without formal knowledge of pedagogy to "make it" in the classroom. Some states have now provided such alternate routes, deliberately bypassing courses in colleges of education. The development of an esoteric knowledge base can only come from sound research provided by competent scholars. There are a lot of studies about teaching and teachers (Dunkin and Biddle, 1974). There are fewer studies dealing with the development of a precise and esoteric theoretical or technical knowledge base in teaching (see Gage, 1979).

The reasons may not be too difficult to deduce. Some research is simply so far out of context to life in schools, it is relatively useless in improving teaching in schools. For research to lead to professionalization it must be able to demonstrate that with its application, teaching consistently improves in real schools over time.

Some teacher scholars continually want to expand what they see in schools to other contexts. Thus their scholarship is about what's wrong with teachers or teaching in schools (Kapferer, 1986). The scholarship and research that is most promising for building an esoteric knowledge base about teaching is confined to schools as we know them. Cuban (1984, p. 268) examined a longitudinal view of what and how teachers have taught between 1890 and 1980 and concluded:

> The variety of what teachers do in classrooms is finite. . . . No longer should the central issue about instruction be: how should teachers teach? . . . I believe the central question is simply: how can what teachers already do be improved?

Most school administrators would undoubtedly agree with Cuban. Most want changes *now* and improvements *now*. But they want them within the current structure of schools as they understand it. That may pose some problems, for there is a scholarly and professional opinion that holds that the teacher's automony must be changed for anything significant to happen (Goodlad, 1984, p. 194).

PROBLEMS WITH STATIC CAREER LADDERS

Creating a model of a senior cadre of teacher leaders in schools without basing it on actual technical mastery of valid pedagogical skills is doomed to fall back on largely bureaucratic rather than instructional benchmarks. So when Boyer (1983) proposes a career hierarchy for teachers, it isn't surprising that he fails to indicate the difference between a career senior teacher and a normal classroom teacher in terms of technical pedagogical skill mastery levels. He forgoes the problem by indicating that a master teacher panel would make the distinction (Boyer, 1983, p. 182). Given the existing incomplete knowledge base of pedagogical growth, not only does Boyer not know, it is highly unlikely that the panel knows either.

Most of the research on these issues is largely nominal in nature; that is, it indicates that some teachers have skill "x" and others don't. Identifying skill "x" on a continuum, enabling a panel to know where one would fall to be called an associate teacher, normal teacher, senior teacher, or master teacher, is far beyond the ability of our current crude measurement and research methods to account for the largest part of what is important in predicting teacher success within these categories.

Most career ladder plans that aim to expand the autonomy of some teachers within the teaching cadre fall back on two lesser qualities of organizational life as the fulcrum for changing some teachers' roles in schools. Those qualities are a longer work year and a larger span of control. Thus senior teachers are paid more, not on the basis of valid and superior technical mastery of pedagogical skills, but on the fact that they work an extra month and supervise or mentor other teachers.

For several reasons, these kinds of career ladders are inadequate as ways to envision the professionalization of teaching as a career. First, they aren't based on skills that are directly applicable to the improvement of instruction and hence pupil learning. If anything, they are much more indirect in nature. Most would be tangential to the teaching-learning process. Second, they change the autonomy of only some teachers and not all teachers—inhibiting the growth of those teachers without much freedom to learn new skills.

Third, they simply add another layer of administration to the existing one and move along extant criteria using the same evaluative instruments already in existence. Given these circumstances, it is highly likely that the best teachers in the public's mind will not be those in the upper rungs of the career ladder, for exactly the same reasons that the best teachers in the system are not principals at the present time. When a career ladder embraces factors other than documented pedagogical abilities and skills, it tends to embrace the criteria of seniority and administration as opposed to technical competence. That means that career ladders neither honor nor promote pedagogical excellence. They are about creating a form without the substance to give it a chance to impact pupils. The rationale is that the best reason to have a career ladder is to have one.

Thus, career ladders offer a confusing rhetoric and picture to the public. When one hears a senior teacher, one may think of a senior physician or senior partner in a law firm. That conjures up the picture of an advanced expert practitioner, not just someone with grey hair or more people to supervise who do the same job. But that is just what most senior teachers will be: older, not necessarily more expert.

The current stair-step career ladder model, copied from the famed Temple City, California, differentiated staffing experiment in the late sixties (English, 1983–84), creates a new rigidity which discourages teacher movement and offers few incentives for those people at the bottom rungs. Once implemented, there is little or no movement in or out of the office holders in the top rungs. If a static career ladder were indeed motivational for teachers at the initial stages of its implementation, what will be motivational after all of the roles are filled and everyone settles into the routine with no hope of advancement because of the lack of movement within the career ladder? Thus, as personnel realize that in reality they are trapped in the bottom rungs for extensive periods of time, there will be an effort to collapse the categories. The same phenomenon occurred in Temple City over twenty years ago. For these teachers, the career ladder is demotivational.

By its very nature the career ladder is shaped like a pyramid. That means that the largest part of the cadre will be at the bottom, with proportionally fewer numbers as one ascends the ladder. If that is true, how can such a model lift the total performance of the cadre, when over half of it is situated at the bottom with little hope of breaking out of the lower rungs?

If, on the other hand, the career ladder were inverted, that is, the bulk of the teachers were master teachers and at the top, then it could be argued that the floor and ceiling of the cadre's performance would be elevated. Which of the state plans for career ladders look like what? The logic of finance allows for only a minority of the teachers to ever be senior or master teachers. The reason is simple: the state can't afford any more.

Thus, career ladder plans have a variety of intrinsic flaws that work against the very goals they were implemented to attain. They were not successful twenty years ago and, unless the flaws are corrected, they will not be successful in the 1980s for the same reasons.

THE PROMISE OF THE CAREER STAGES CONCEPT

The career stages concept is not first and foremost a salary model for teachers. It is not advanced as a way out of the dilemma of discovering a new tactic for raising teachers' salaries that doesn't sound like the same old tune for weary state legislators. Furthermore, it isn't a new evaluation system. Rather, it is an approach to improving and sustaining teacher motivation for teaching within schools over time. Many of the precepts that underlie the career stages concept have been known for some time. They aren't new in that sense.

For example, Hall (1966, p. 88) examined the stages of a professional career in medicine. He identified four distinct stages. They are: (1) generating the ambition to become a doctor; (2) gaining admittance to a medical school; (3) acquiring a clientele; and (4) developing an informal set of relationships with colleagues.

Hall's model is directly concerned with the internal perceptions and feelings of medical doctors only at stages one and four when the aspiring physician centers on medicine as his or her life goal and develops sustaining relationships with colleagues. What causes one to want to become a doctor? Interestingly, data have been gathered on medical careers to find out. A study of 704 doctors indicated that the single greatest motivational factor was the influence of the family (Johnson, 1983).

Career studies of teachers are harder to come by, yet there are some data about it. Kaufman (1984) did a superb analysis of the records of some 250 women of an estimated 600 who were sent west to teach in the U.S. in the decade following 1846. The records were obtained from the National Board of Popular Education. By and large, these single, eastern women who went west to teach were motivated by the need to support themselves, some at an early age, in one of the few respectable occupations then open to women. Kaufman (1984, p. 15) indicates that many were eldest daughters who, because of a variety of factors, soon became socially too old for marriage.

My model of career stages begins with the anticipatory because that is where most administrators in most school systems look at entry teaching. The concept could be expanded rather easily in the future to include the motivational factors that induce young people to pursue teaching in college and enter the profession as a career. It would be entirely consistent with the idea of basing career stages on internal factors impacting career orientation throughout a complete teaching career.

RELATED RESEARCH ON THE "PASSAGES" IDEA

Other data that professionals go through a kind of "passages" phenomenon have been presented by Guy (1985) in her study of medical personnel at two different hospitals. The factors that influenced the passages or stages were policies of selection pursued by the hospital, the dominant culture of the institution, and the interaction of the two over time on the individual. Guy examines these interactions under the rubric of "longevity" in one place of work.

In a descriptive notation of her findings, closely paralleling the major thesis of this book for teachers, Guy (1985, p. 133) notes, "changes in preferences occur in a cyclical fashion among staff according to their general career life span with the organization." Guy (1985, p. 133) describes the series of interactive events as follows:

(1) A person enters the organization with his or her own set of preferences.
(2) After a period of time in which the person interacts with colleagues, the preference structure changes.
(3) The new preference structure "freezes" for awhile, however.
(4) The altered preference structure "thaws" and changes in interaction with the job and the person's career goals.
(5) The altered preference structure is revised and refreezes again for a time.

According to Guy this cycle is endlessly repeated within organizations.

The career stages concept for classroom teachers has also indicated that within this cycle for teachers, the effect of movement can be positive or negative to the school or the school district, and positive or destructive to the teacher personally.

Clues as to what may be a causative factor or factors in schools that impact changes in such cycles has been the subject of review by Phillips (1982). Phillips cites a report by the Mayo Clinic (UNESCO, 1954) that within a study of professionals complaining of physical problems, compared to clergy, lawyers, and dentists, teachers had the highest number of neurotic complaints (p. 186).

The two major concerns in the school environment that seem to account for such complaints are loneliness and anxiety. These two interacting pressures have led people like Brodsky (1977) to consider teaching to be one of the most stressful of all occupations (Phillips, 1982, p. 192).

The cause of loneliness is the isolation of the classroom teacher from the structure of most schools. As the teacher confronts ever more rebellious students, wider ranges of diversity among pupils, and increasing bureaucratic and impersonal rules, the sense of isolation, of growing impotence and helplessness is provoked.

The cause of anxiety, according to Phillips, is discipline. The requirement to maintain order in the classroom is overpowering and always present. This means that teachers function under constant, total, and continuing tension. Such unrelenting tension can lead to physiological or somatic complaints, psychological problems of depression, self-doubt, and nervousness, and social problems of withdrawal, work absence, turnover, and burnout (Phillips, 1982, p. 189). The effects of anxiety have been well documented for over fifty years in teaching. Hicks (1933) discovered in a survey of some 600 teachers that 17 percent suffered from nervous breakdowns.

The twin pressures of being alone and under constant tension present teachers with a job situation of unresolved conflict. In short, they perceive to be trapped. Brodsky (1977) compared the amount of stress to being overexposed to certain types of radioactive materials, "We should inform teachers . . . and others who are subject to long-term stress about the early indicators of overexposure" (p. 138, Phillips, 1982, p. 193).

These pressures are substantially intensified when one considers the level of violence that exists in some school systems. Phillips (1982, p. 197) indicates that in 1979 *The New York Times* reported that in the New York City schools alone, there were 1,856 assults, 1,097 robberies, 310 fires, 1,243 cases of disorderly conduct, 69 cases of sexual abuse, and over 300 cases involving deadly weapons of one sort or another in just one year. Teaching is not only lonely and stressful, but also very dangerous as well. Few other occupations must function in such conditions.

The career stages model takes into account the teacher's internal status, orientation to work, colleague interactions, and classroom performance to place a teacher at a particular growth stage. Productivity is not related to hierarchical position so much as it is directly related to the teacher's current perceptions and preferences within the school in which he or she is currently working. Productivity is inherently contextual and very site specific. Except in the case of deep withdrawal, it is changeable. This approach to examining teaching careers appears to be far more realistic about the actual conditions teachers face in schools day in and day out, and therefore, it is far more powerful to impact changes in the work teachers actually perform in schools. Static hierarchies simply encapsulate these problems. By recognizing that a teacher's role orientation is fluid and interactive in his or her career lifetime, one avoids enshrining job de-motivators, and incorporates work motivators for the largest part of the teaching cadre for the longest time they are actually teaching in the schools.

CHANGING THE TEACHER'S ROLE
IN SCHOOLS-EMPOWERMENT

Empowerment is one of the new education "in" words of the late 1980s. It has yet to acquire a precise definition. However, one thing is quite certain; its adherents mean change in the role, and more importantly, the autonomy of teachers in schools.

Autonomy has long been considered one of the benchmarks of a true profession (Friedson, 1984). Yet, autonomy must be accompanied by expertise and a credential. Friedson (1984, p. 14) stated:

> Whatever else they are, professionals are experts: indeed, "profession" as opposed to "amateur" connotes not only earning a living by one's work, but also superior skillfulness, or expertise at doing a professional as opposed to an amateurish job.

In this sense, the career stages model would assume that the expert/master teacher is a professional. Yet none of the teachers can be a professional without a deep consideration of autonomy.

Professional autonomy has several dimensions. The first dimension is one that relates to an occupational monopoly. This means that those in the profession control who enters it. It also includes a political monopoly which refers only to members of the profession being able to serve as authoritative spokespersons to guide laws and rules bearing on its performance. Last, autonomy means that the profession determines and controls its own work standards and rules (Friedson, 1984, p. 21).

Upon examination, teaching fails rather noticeably on all three dimensions. Teachers do not control their own profession in matters of entry and discipline. The spokespersons of national teacher associations or unions do not have the last word on the performance of the cadre. And finally, teachers do not solely direct their own work standards. It is true that teacher associations/unions do influence laws and policies regarding their work, though that influence has not been very persuasive or powerful in the eight years of the Reagan administration.

Collective bargaining has led to the imposition of union control or at least influence on some working conditions in the schools. Yet, in no case do teachers have the final word on many important issues concerning the work they must perform in the schools. Clearly on any dimension regarding the issue of autonomy, teachers do not prevail. In order to examine what that means, let us change the situation to explore a concept useful in other professions, i.e., that of a professional practice. In schools there is practice teaching but no teaching practice.

Autonomy Reconsidered: A Teaching Practice

Think about the last time you visited a physician, lawyer, or accountant. You probably went to an office after making an appointment. Then you explained your problem or need to the professional who responded. At that time the professional indicated what he or she believed might suffice, or indicated the possibility of a referral. There may be some review of records or additional diagnosis involved. At the same time, you as a patient or client were deciding whether or not you liked this person and wanted to continue the relationship. Autonomy therefore existed on both sides of this potential relationship. At the conclusion of the meeting, you went to the professional's secretary or billing officer and paid a fee for the visitation. Depending upon the nature of the exchange, this relationship may continue, or it may not. As a client or patient, you may come back to this professional, you may be referred to another professional, or you may seek out still another professional for a variety of reasons.

Suppose there were no state supported schools as they are known now. Suppose all schools were entrepreneurial. If schooling were required, one would look up a school in a phone book or ask friends if they know of any good schools. Then one would go to make inquiries.

The scenario fits the mode of private schools today. It is not accurate for most public schools, except perhaps for some magnet schools in districts undergoing desegregation experiences. Most public schools have a "captive" clientele. They are therefore freed from much energy in securing a clientele in order to stay in business. Such guaranteed schools don't have to worry about things like market development or practice development (Wilson, 1984).

Now let's proceed into the school. A teaching practice would mean that a group of teachers had banded together out of common interest and some common expertise to offer their services within a school. Again, they were free to accept or reject the students based upon their judgment and professional expertise. There would have to be some intake procedure to determine the fit for the professional services to be rendered. If the teachers felt their services were not appropriate, the client would be referred to one that was appropriate.

Thus, the teachers are firmly in control of which and how prospective students are selected.

If the reader is a teacher, he or she may be smiling to him/herself, and thinking, "That would be real control." However, the price for such autonomy is high. It would also mean that with no guaranteed clientele, one's income would be geared to the marketplace. In effect, we would have an almost perfect voucher plan in operation.

In truth, few teachers want that much autonomy. What they want is a kind of guaranteed clientele within a school where their autonomy is enhanced. That means that the concept of a teaching practice has to be modified. A more accurate model might be that of the health plan equivalent of an HMO (Health Maintenance Organization). In the HMO, a patient receives lower medical costs in a trade-off for the right to select one's personal physician. In exchange for this forfeiture, doctors are freed from the necessity of practice development and marketing because they no longer have to worry about keeping up a steady stream of patients. Doctors also have a higher degree of flexibility with their own time because patients understand that they may be shifted around a bit in emergencies. That simply is how an HMO works.

A school might work that way, too. When one speaks of autonomy, one is referring to a greater degree of control over what one does in one's workplace. And it means the right of refusal within certain guidelines. Thus, a teacher or group of teachers would decide among themselves how best to group students, when, where, and how and inform a scheduler of their decisions. The school schedule would be driven by teacher-based decisions, not decisions made by the administrator in the front office or a guidance counselor.

Teachers would decide what curricula were most appropriate to fit the state's criteria for graduation and parcel out their expertise in the pieces of the curricula that matched their interests and abilities accordingly. Teachers would determine the sequencing of the curriculum and arrange for its appropriate delivery and monitoring. Teachers would determine the nature of grades or student evaluations. Teachers would select texts, perhaps write their own, and decide about the most effective form of instruction.

This scenario is not an exercise in romance or fancy. Some teachers in some places actually do this now. In large high schools, teachers often enjoy these decisions. But the price is always that teachers assume more accountability and visibility for those same decisions.

Thus, as teachers make more decisions, they become more vulnerable at the same time. And if they make the final decision, they become totally responsible for the outcome of that decision. That means that comparable to administrators who often make such decisions now, teachers can be sued for engaging in practices that are illegal or unethical, whereas now, some principals decide on the nature of pupil punishment and can get sued; if teachers assume that responsibility, their legal vulnerability also shifts concomitantly.

So autonomy isn't all a bed of roses. It won't ever be, "Let us make all the decisions and leave us alone." In a public bureaucracy with a captive clientele, the people who make the decisions are accountable for them. Any school administrator will inform you that in the last ten years the vulnerability of the administration has increased along with the paperwork. If teachers think they now have a lot of paperwork, an improved level of autonomy will also be accompanied by more paperwork. This aspect of empowerment is seldom discussed because many of the advocates have never experienced the kind of decision making routinely executed by most school administrators today. Empowerment means increased autonomy. It also means one's actions are subject to greater public scrutiny and outright intrusion by public regulatory agencies and parents with lawyers. The only way to avoid public regulation is to practice one's profession outside a professional bureaucracy in private and live or die on the vagaries of the marketplace.

Teachers can't have it both ways. If they want to exercise more control within schools over their work, they also have to assume more responsibility and liability for the quality of that work. Administrators are often blamed for the poor quality of teaching in some schools. When and if school administrators are removed from the realm of decision making in schools in which they exercise some judgment now, teachers will be alone in facing that same public criticism. It comes with the turf.

It is the opinion of the author that teachers can, should, and must assume greater control over their work. The knowledge base of teaching has expanded to enable them to do so. It is also the opinion of the author that the assumption of control must be firmly anchored in the professional knowlege base, and not in some bureaucratically contrived career ladder. Such artifacts will fold up easily when funding dies out, or when the authority of the state can no longer prop them up by forcing them on teachers or the public.

LEADERSHIP IN SCHOOLS

Even as teachers' roles are evolving towards the assumption of duties and tasks now largely administrative and controlling, the function of leadership will always exist in a school. If administrators are little more than bureaucrats filling in blanks of paper for inter-agency articulation or scheduling buses or assemblies, they can be replaced. If that's all that school administration is, such services can be purchased at a considerably lower rate than what most school districts now pay for them. If, however, school administration is about leadership, then it has a bright future in our schools. In fact, without such leadership, teachers and teaching will not go far apace from where it is today.

Consider a recent study by Blase (1987) in which he examined effective school leadership through the eyes of teachers. This was a study not based on standardized achievement test data or work analyses of the tasks of principals, but was based on teacher descriptions garnered with a two and one-half year case study (1983–1986). The researcher collected voluminous data of seventy-five to eighty teachers, compiling detailed work histories of their careers. Many of these teachers had experienced a lot of principals, at least 125 different principals to be exact (Blase, 1987, p. 592).

When the data were placed into a context allowing a thematic analysis, Blase discerned two realms of leadership of principals. The first was task-relevant competencies, and the second consisted of staff consideration competencies. Blase's study is very consistent with the themes reiterated in this book. Effective principals were those who were supportive of teachers in regard to parental and student conflicts, developed doable channels in which teachers expressed their expertise and feelings, recognized the professional and personal rights of all teachers, and offered praise and appreciation to both teachers individually and to the faculty as a whole. Effective principals also delegated authority. The result of the actions of effective principals in the eyes of teachers were increases in morale, cooperation, faculty cohesiveness, and trust, as well as group problem-solving and communication abilities (Blase, 1987, p. 596). When the consideration dimensions were coupled with superb task competencies, they resulted in decreased student discipline problems, as well as diminished uncertainty and conflict. They also resulted in an increase in teacher involvement, time on task, problem-solving effectiveness, and teacher expectations for student achievement. There was also an increase in hopefulness about attaining goals (Blase, 1987, p. 595).

In short, Blase's study has confirmed and codified what many seasoned and reflective school administrators and teachers have known all along.

SUMMARY

There has been much talk about professionalizing teaching. Given the nature of teaching in public bureaucracies, it is unlikely that professionalization will occur in the same fashion as in the occupations of law, medicine, or accounting.

There is considerable debate as to whether or not the knowledge base of teaching is adequate for full professionalization to occur. That discussion is of considerable importance to the central issue of the autonomy of teachers in schools. Without a clear and consistent base of esoteric knowledge which discretely separates an amateur from a professional, autonomy cannot be rooted in expertise. Without that condition, professionalization cannot rest upon the authority of superior skills or knowledge. The heart of any claim to professionalization must begin here.

Many models of career ladders are oblivious to the dimensions cited in Blase's work. They are more intent on creating a senior cadre of teachers not rooted in classroom expertise, though many have tried to ferret out such competence on exams, standardized tests, or even teacher constructed portfolios. Their record to date is not very promising. Indeed, the career ladder concept may be an idea without an adequate knowledge/research base to give it any hope of operational legitimacy or longevity in the schools for some time to come.

The career stages concept can be applied now, because it is consistent with the extant knowledge base and practice in the schools about what makes an effective educational site. Furthermore, its precepts can be traced to what those studying the peculiar problems of teachers have been saying about teaching in the past 100 years.

INQUIRY

Questions and Answers About Chapter Nine

Question #1: *You refer to the fact that there isn't a sufficient knowledge base for the professionalization of teaching. What has to change for this to occur?*

Answer: More research on the issue is required. We very much need the presence of sound, context-relevant scholarship. This means that rather than using context-free probes, the attack by scholars has to be on what separates teaching performance in real classrooms. In my opinion there are too few researchers who have had a sound and recent knowledge base about teaching or administration in schools. Tacit knowledge is that which often cannot be directly translated into quantifiable relationships, but is important as a way to direct inquiry. I see some scholars completely abandoning external searches for teacher characteristics, looking for how teachers themselves think about such things. We do know some things about good teaching, but what we know is not of sufficient depth to qualify teaching as a profession. We will not grow very much until we can be more specific about what makes teaching special, other than a calling to engage in a nurturing relationship.

Question #2: *You seem to be quite critical of career ladders. Do you see anything good about them at all?*

Answer: Yes. They have raised the public awareness of some of the poor working conditions in schools, they have helped somewhat in raising the pay of teachers, though not nearly enough, and they have ushered in some forms of improved staff development programs. But that won't be enough to maintain the career ladders. My fear is that at the same time we have raised public awareness, we have raised public expectations beyond that which we can reasonably attain, and we will suffer another form of public disapproval. If that takes the avenue of decreased public support, we will hurt ourselves rather badly.

Question #3: *Do you really think there can ever be a school without a principal?*

Answer: Of course. But I don't realistically see one functioning very well within the current educational milieu. The state structure of education is far too authoritarian to permit it because almost all forms of accountability legislation are "top down." That approach reinforces the centrality of administration and it doesn't make any difference if the principal exists or not. Someone in the school will have to be responsible for replying. My fear is that if principals were removed, a lead teacher would soon become a principal again via the immense internal socialization forces for control that dominate most school systems in most states. Within our current environment a leaderless school would be out of business. Principalship, or some role like it, is necessary to survive in public education today.

Question #4: *How many principals do you know who are really competent to be instructional leaders?*

Answer: Not nearly enough. The need is most acute at the secondary school, most particularly at the high school. I see the fewest number of principals at this level capable of doing the job when it comes to curriculum and instruction. And too many function within the authoritarian role model of coach to players. The high school principalship has for too long been the almost exclusive domain of "the good old boys" from the athletic department.

Question #5: *Do you really think that teachers want to be administrators and put up with all the pressure and paperwork so commonplace in school administration?*

Answer: Yes and no. Teachers aren't excited about more paperwork, and they aren't excited about more pressure. Neither are administrators. I think many teachers would accept those deficits, however, to gain increased autonomy in schools. It's kind of like growing up. Teenagers want only the fun part of adulthood. When they think about their freedom, they don't think about paying bills, mortgages, and taxes or going to work every day for forty or fifty years. They think only about having fun and doing what one wants to do. But being an adult means taking on all the responsibilities. Teachers can do it; it's time they did.

REFERENCES

BLASE, J. "Dimensions of Effective School Leadership: The Teacher's Perspective," *American Educational Research Journal,* 24, pp. 589–610 (Winter, 1987).

BOYER, E. *High School.* New York:Harper and Row Publishers (1983).

BRODSKY, C. "Long-Term Stress in Teachers and Prison Guards," *Journal of Occupational Medicine,* 19, pp. 133–138 (1977).

CUBAN, L. *How Teachers Taught.* New York:Longman (1984).

DUNKIN, M. and B. Biddle. *The Study of Teaching.* New York:Holt, Rinehart, Winston (1974).

ENGLISH, F. "Merit Pay: Reflections on Education's Lemon Tree," *Educational Leadership,* 41, pp. 72–79 (December, January, 1983–84).

FRIEDSON, E. "The Theory of Professions: State of the Art." In *The Sociology of the Professions,* R. Dingwall and P. Lewis (eds.). New York:St. Martin's Press, 19–37 (1983).

GAGE, N. "The Generality of Dimensions of Teaching." In *Research on Teaching,* P. Peterson and H. Walberg (eds.). Berkeley, California:McCutchan Publishing Corporation, 264–269 (1979).

GOODLAD, J. *A Place Called School.* New York:McGraw-Hill Book Company (1984).

GUY, M. *Professionals in Organizations.* New York:Praeger Publishers (1985).

HALL, O. "Stages in a Professional Career." In *Professionalization,* H. Vollmer and D. Mills (eds.). Englewood Cliffs, New Jersey:Prentice Hall, 87–97 (1966).

HICKS, F. *The Mental Health of Teachers.* New York:Cullman and Ghertner (1933).

JOHNSON, M. "Professional Careers and Biographies." In *The Sociology of the Professions,* R. Dingwall and P. Lewis (eds.). New York:St. Martin's Press, 242–262 (1983).

KAPFERER, J. "Curricula and the Reproduction of Structured Social Inequalities," *Curriculum Inquiry*, 15, pp. 5–32 (Spring, 1986).

KAUFMAN, P. *Women Teachers on the Frontier*. New Haven:Yale University Press (1984).

OLSON, L. "Teaching's Knowledge Base Seen Still Elusive," *Education Week*, 7, p. 7 (March 2, 1988).

PHILLIPS, E. *Stress, Health, and Psychological Problems in the Major Professions*. Washington, D.C.: University Press of America (1982).

United Nations Education, Scientific and Cultural Organization. "Highest Neurosis Found in Teachers," *UNESCO Courier*, 5, 25 (1954).

WILSON, A. *Practice Development for Professional Firms*. London:McGraw-Hill Book Company (1984).

Putting the Career Stages Model Into Practice

THE KEY ACTIVITY IS RENEWAL

THE beauty of applying the career stages model in an ongoing school district is that it doesn't take any new labels, hoopla, or elaborate negotiations to implement it. In fact, it is better if none of these conditions are present. The school administration is supposed to do what it can to create the working conditions that will inspire and lead the teaching cadre. Now, with the career stages model as a conceptual framework, the administration and board set forth to deliberately raise the performance of its classroom teachers.

The key activity is renewal. Professional and personal renewal is the life blood, the force that moves it, the activity that regenerates it again and again. Renewal is a never-ending pursuit. The end is the means. The pursuit of excellence is the reward.

The critical assumption is that nearly all humans want to keep up the pursuit, want to achieve, want to be recognized, want the best! Creating the conditions that enable nearly all teachers to be winners is what school administration is all about. It's what some strategists would call a win-win situation.

Robert Waterman, in his book *The Renewal Factor* (1987, pp. 15–16), summarizes the relationship most succinctly, "The essence of living, really living, is renewal. Without renewal there can be no excellence."

The critical observation is that change is the only thing one can count on. People change, the work environment changes, the administration changes. Renewal and change are one and the same. Variability is what life in organizations is about. Yet, the administration is almost always charged with reducing variability and monitoring stability.

195

Renewal as a major force means recognizing the power of change to stimulate and maintain a healthy, vibrant level of teaching in the schools. To do this, the school administration will have to re-examine its commitment to maintaining the routine, particularly the bureaucratic priorities on minute, petty rules, the rigidity, and the formalization. The red tape has to be reduced, the paperwork diminished. In short, some ambiguity has to be re-inserted into the workplace. A new balance has to be defined between activities that lead to stability and those that lead to change.

Of course, a school in anarchy is neither creative nor renewing. In that case, teachers and administrators are struggling to survive and have no energy or incentive to ponder renewal. Renewal takes place in an atmosphere of structured informality. Spontaneity is built in, rather than stamped out, and spontaneity is rewarded and recognized. That leads to other possibilities of incorporating renewal in schools based on eight indices developed by Waterman (1987).

INFORMED OPPORTUNISM

There is no one way to put a teacher into renewal; there are hundreds of ways. The administrator who can do it has two characteristics. He/she knows the staff well, individual by individual, and he/she has a general sense of where the organization is going so that when an opportunity for renewal comes, it meets not only the needs of the individual for growth, but also the needs of the system for change in a specific direction (see also Grace, Buser, and Stuck, 1987).

When these two are linked together and supported by the administration, the rate of change is accelerated. I've seen a brand new K–12 Student Assistance program go from an idea to an institutional program in less than twelve months because these two characteristics were present.

To make it work, the administrator must have a personal relationship with each staff member. He/she must know them as human beings: imperfect and vulnerable but wanting to do well. This is not to say the administrator must like each staff member or be a personal friend to each one. That wouldn't work either. But the administrator must know enough about what makes the teacher tick, that he/she is cognizant of what general type of activity will renew the individual.

In the case of the Student Assistance program, the twenty-five people initially involved represented the guidance staff, nursing staff, teachers who were particularly sensitive to the holistic needs of students, and administrators who viewed solving some of the personal, social problems of students as a means of improving student achievement.

These people did not come collectively to the administrator and say that involvement in a Student Assistance program would be a renewing activity for them, but because the administrator had a sense of the orientation of these people, it turned out to be just that.

Because the people involved found the experience renewing, the period of time necessary to implement the program was short, and the willingness of the people involved to stick in there during the hard times was evident.

How an administrator goes about getting to know his/her staff in this humanistic way can take many routes. A stroll through the building early in the morning to chat with teachers works for some. Periodically, stopping in the teachers' room for an early morning cup of coffee is another. Sharing food somehow supports the development of personal rapport among all staff. Coffees, lunches, and afternoon snacks all offer opportunities for people to get to know one another on a personal level.

When a staff member has a severe personal problem like a pending divorce or a severe illness in the family, the administration usually knows about it. The administration should be supportive, but it needs to become aware of the positive things going on in the life of the staff as well.

THE NECESSITY FOR STRATEGIC PLANNING

Supporting renewal activities that fit into the improvement of the total building or district requires the administrator to have a vision for where the district is headed. Involving staff in the strategic planning process can provide the district with this vision and identify many avenues for individual renewal (Ansoff, 1979).

The strategic planning process begins with a description of where the district is now, content area by content area and building by building. It is recommended that this process include not only a description of what is, but a statement of tangible indicators of achievement and a listing of weaknesses.

The second step in this strategic planning process is to choose a broader planning horizon (Naisbitt, 1982). Then dream, speculate, and reach a general consensus about what the system would look like at that time, content area by content area, building by building (English and Steffy, 1982).

Once accomplished, this broader vision for the future provides the parameters for staff renewal activities.

It is essential that the administration does not allow the future vision to become locked in stone. Forecasting the future is tricky business. Nothing is certain or forever. The strategic planning process is fine as long as everyone keeps it in perspective. The process of involving staff in this visionary thinking is often more valuable than the end being specified. The system must remain fluid at all times. Administrators must have their antennae up and be alert for opportunities to link an idea with a person to promote renewal. They are there. More opportunities exist than there is time to support. At the end of each day, an administrator should ask him/herself, "How have I helped the system renew itself today?"

Leaders who have the ability to sense opportunity where others cannot are leaders who produce system and individual renewal. They recognize the opportunity the moment it occurs. They recognize a tiny spark which can become a strongly burning torch. They not only recognize it, but also provide the encouragement and support to make it burn.

DIRECTION AND EMPOWERMENT

Feeling in charge of one's destiny is a key component of renewal. Waterman (1987) has termed it empowerment. Many refer to it as the ability to participate in the decision-making process. Whatever it is called, it means that within the boundaries set by the system, the individual has control over his/her environment. For renewal to be effective, this control must be sufficient for the individual teacher to feel in command of his/her own situation.

Empowerment may take the form of being responsible for the development of a budget to support a new program. It may mean the selection of materials, the design of lesson plans, the allocation of instructional time, or the development of an assessment system. It may be any one of these or all of them depending on what the renewal activity is.

The point is that the individual in renewal has to be empowered to make the decisions necessary to sustain the renewal. Frequently, the administration wants not only to dictate the area of renewal, but also to manage every aspect of it. The result may be renewal for the administration, but withdrawal for the teacher.

This doesn't mean that the administration has to give teachers a free rein in the renewal process. It is the role of the administration to set the parameters for renewal. These parameters may be financial constraints, such as requiring that the renewal project may not cost more than $100 for new supplies. They may be in release time for the teacher, who may not be permitted to use more than two release time days to visit other schools or receive training.

Whatever the parameters, they should be clearly stated up front so the teacher anticipating renewal activity can plan accordingly. Teachers are just as flexible as students when it comes to getting used to the leadership style of an administrator. The administrator can be authoritarian or democratic. Teachers will accommodate accordingly. What they can't tolerate is being told they have the freedom to do something and then being told otherwise.

When teachers are given direction and empowerment, the creative juices start to flow. They know the success or failure of the program is in their hands. They also know that the administrator had enough faith in them to give them this freedom. Teachers placed in this position will put forth tremendous effort to see that the project works, especially if they had the idea for the project in the beginning.

One systematic way to support teacher renewal activities is through the development of yearly professional improvement plans. In the state of New Jersey, the type of planning is mandated by the state. Every professional staff person in every district in the state is supposed to develop a Professional Improvement Plan (PIP) in May. The plan is reviewed by the administration and finalized in October. Both the administrator and the teacher can contribute to the plan.

In some districts the PIP is used by the administration to identify areas in which the teacher needs to improve. Sometimes the PIP includes building or district goals. However, the PIP should always include renewal goals for the teacher. As we can see, not only are the goals stated, but also the activities to be accomplished to reach the goals, who is responsible for completing each of the activities, and when each of the activities is to be accomplished.

During the year, periodic conferences are held to review the progress made toward meeting the goals. At the end of the year, the PIP becomes the basis for part of the teacher's yearly evaluation.

Another way to support renewal activities for teachers is to encourage teachers to submit applications for mini-grants. The amount of money attached to each mini-grant need not be large. Grants of $200 are common. In a district of 2500 students with an annual budget of $14 million, the possibility of ten or twelve mini-grants does not seem unreasonable.

If the district is interested in promoting the use of micro-computers in the classroom, mini-grants may be made available for just this type of project. The possibilities are limitless. With the administration providing the direction and the teachers empowered, the opportunity for system renewal is vastly enhanced.

FRIENDLY FACTS, CONGENIAL CONTROLS

How many teachers learn that their system is doing well, or not so well, in a certain basic skills area by reading about it in the paper? Too many! When this happens, it can be because information is not shared freely in the system.

Teachers should be informed about the good news and the bad news. They can handle it. It may just be that a teacher has an idea of how to correct the problem, whether it's low achievement scores, high student dropout rates, or the number of student suspensions.

Usually the person closest to the problem has the clearest idea of what it is, its causes, and some of the possible solutions. The administrator who encourages teachers to come up with creative solutions is the administrator who supports renewal.

Of course the controls are there, too. There are always limitations on the array of possibilities for solving any problem. The most obvious one is financial. All systems are limited in the amount of dollar resources available. Frequently, the classroom teacher is completely removed from the budget development process. All that the teachers know is that the new piece of equipment they wanted has been cut from the budget. The reason for the cut seems clear to them. The central administration doesn't value what they are doing. After all, no one spoke to them about the cut. If they had been asked about the priority of the item, the teachers would have been glad to cut another area in order to get this important article. By failing to involve the classroom teachers in the development of the budget and by failing to explain the entire budget to the faculty, the district widens the possibility of misunderstanding and fosters suspicion between the administration and the staff (see Cibulka, 1987).

Budgets can be congenial controls if information is shared freely between the administration, the board, and the staff. The budget is a public document. There should be no secrets about it. Comparisons and analysis from year to year are readily available in the business manager's office. The procedures used to communicate about the budget can make teachers perceive it as a friendly fact and a congenial control or as a punitive reprisal. The choice is up to the way the administration decides to handle the situation.

Even more limiting to the decision-making process in schools is the amount of allotted instructional time available. Each year brings new demands on time. The addition of citizenship education, career education, AIDS education, environmental education, ethnic education, and computer education are just a few of the add-ons to the curriculum in the past few years. At the same time, there has been no noticeable increase in the amount of instructional time available. Too often, little is known about how instructional time decisions are being made. The staff knows that the high school operates on eight forty-five minute periods and that the school day begins at 8:00 A.M., and ends at 2:15 P.M. (see Keefe, 1987).

One quick solution for declining math achievement scores is for the administration to unilaterally increase the amount of instructional time in math by reducing the amount of physical education instruction. If the information had been shared with the teachers, they may have come up with a better solution like modifying group practices or securing some supplemental materials to correct a particular deficiency. These kinds of solutions are only possible when the teachers who really understand the problem are involved in the solution.

In the cooperative decision-making process, facts become friendly and controls congenial. No one objects to congenial controls if they are stated honestly and are not used as an excuse for why something can't be changed. Congenial controls can be the challenge which causes teachers to become surprisingly creative. Districts promoting the honest exchange of information, the good news and the bad news, help create a climate for renewal in the system.

A DIFFERENT MIRROR

There is comfort in routine. Routines are necessary for schools to function. Can one imagine the chaos which would be created if 850 fifth, sixth, and seventh graders showed up one day and didn't know where to go, how long to stay there, or what to do? On the other hand, can one imagine the level of enthusiasm generated by the teacher who arrives at 7:45 A.M., parks in the same spot, enters the same room, and begins the same lesson every year on the fifteenth day of school? The lesson will be taught five times that day. And this is the fifteenth year the process has been repeated.

Breaking old habits is difficult, but renewal cannot take place without it. Somehow the cycle has to be interrupted. This is the role of the visionary leader. The effective leader should provide the system with stability and support, but he/she also needs to continuously shake the system just a little. This presence of gentle tension can keep the system alive, alert, and open to new ideas.

Leadership for renewal is not maintenance leadership. Leadership for renewal is leadership that is characterized as being curious, inquisitive, and willing to look at the organization through different colored glasses. It is leadership which listens, and leadership which actively solicits constructive criticism.

Most educators have had the experience of going off to a convention and coming back filled with new ideas. They have been opened to the possibility for renewal. All of this enthusiasm quickly fades if the environment to which the educator is returning is not one which supports renewal. Often there is no follow-up at all on the part of the administration. At the very least, the teacher should be asked to write a report about the experience, which requires him/her to indicate the possibilities for renewal generated by it. This report need not be very long. It can be used to share ideas with other staff members who were not able to attend.

It has been noted that teaching is a lonely profession. Teachers are isolated from one another. The combination of isolation and routine is deadly. Frequently, the only thing that breaks this lethal cycle is a crisis. In a crisis situation, we all tend to look at the problem and see things we overlooked before. To renew organizations, one should not have to rely on a crisis to occur. For renewing organizations, curiosity is an institutional attribute (Waterman, 1987).

Systems can get bogged down in their own "group think." When teams of people work together for long periods of time, the behavior patterns of each member of the team becomes well-known to all. Everyone knows who is likely to speak first or who will have supportive comments to make and who will voice criticism. It is also well-known whose suggestions will most likely be followed. The habitual nature of the group-think process can be so reduced to a routine that it is self-defeating and leads to maintaining the status quo, rather than opening the system to possibilities of renewal.

Whatever the routines, they ought to be modified from time to time. Invite a known critic of the system to attend meetings in which administrators are making decisions. Ask the person for feedback about what they saw. Listen to his/her comments. Try altering the composition of decision-making teams. Include students and parents intermittently. Open a meeting periodically to the entire faculty and use it as a meet-and-talk exchange.

Try to maintain a balance in the hiring practices by including a combination of locals and cosmopolitans. Seek a teaching cadre with vastly different training experiences and life experiences.

Encourage teacher visitations within your own system. Hire a substitute for a day and allow a teacher to visit another district which is known to have an exemplary program. Build cooperative coalitions among neighboring school districts. Plan cooperative in-service programs together. Share a teacher.

Offer teachers an opportunity to exchange teaching positions for a year. The teacher exchange should be jointly approved by the teachers and the administrators involved. At the end of the year, the teachers would go back to their original assignments. Teachers tend not to request transfers because they don't want a permanent change. Offer them the opportunity to look through the idealistic cyce of the anticipatory teacher for a year to stimulate renewal.

All of these suggestions help build a school climate where risk-taking behavior is supported. Educators ask students to take risks every day in every class, such as learning new skills, trying out those skills in front of their peers, and being evaluated on how effectively the skill was performed. Teachers should be encouraged to do the same thing.

For students, we call it developing a love of learning. There has to be a way for teachers to engage in activities designed to foster the pursuit of this love of learning. Without it, atrophy, stagnation, and withdrawal seep into the attitude and behavior of the teacher and the ethos of the system.

TEAMWORK, TRUST, POLITICS, AND POWER

Teamwork in a renewing district doesn't mean simply that the teachers, the administrators, or the board are operating as a team. What it means is that everyone in the system is operating as a team. Everyone in the system has accepted responsibility for the success of the system and has a degree of ownership for making the system work. This type of teamwork takes years to develop. The foundation for this type of teamwork is the development of mutually acceptable goals toward which everyone is working.

The game of "gotcha" is not played in systems where teamwork is functioning. When there is a cooperative effort among the board, the administration, the staff, the support personnel, the students, and the community, there are few goals the system cannot accomplish. However, it is virtually impossible for a system to meet the idiosyncratic needs of boards, the staff, or the parents in isolation from the rest of the system because satisfying them involves changing the whole system in some way.

Teamwork is based on mutual trust and respect. It begins with the acceptance of the principle that humans are basically good and trustworthy and that most of the people in the system are working toward the good of the system. It means focusing on what is good in the system and trying to solve the problems which may be causing difficulty.

It means accepting the information in the system as truthful and not designed to hide the truth or discredit subgroups in the organization.

For administrators, it means dealing with people in open, trustful, forthright ways. Problems are unavoidable in complex systems like school districts. In fact, most administrators admit to at least three types of problems: people problems, people problems, and people problems (Black and English, 1986). Unionism seems to have accentuated the basic mistrust between teachers and management. The period of decreasing student enrollment has added to the problem. During the past few years, the entire profession has been under attack by segments of the general public. The situation has been exacerbated by the numerous national reports. The time has come for a new initiative in cooperation. The teaching profession, for the most part, is well-trained, mature, and experienced. Teachers may not make the first move toward this cooperative relationship, but administrators can and must, for the continued rebirth and renewal of the profession.

Schooling is a political business. From the hiring of the new superintendent to the naming of the football coach to the development and enforcement of the new suspension policy, politics plays a role.

Education is now playing a significant role in national politics. Few state governors are being elected today without clearly stating their position on education. The image the general public has of the public schools is not a good one. It is perceived that educators are content to graduate many students after twelve or thirteen years of instruction who are not equipped with the necessary skills to handle entry level work. Newspapers appear to take sheer delight in publishing stories depicting the ineptitude of students and teachers. When it comes to raising school taxes or passing a school referendum, taxpayers are quick to take out their frustration about the perceived deficiencies of the system by defeating the proposals.

Each new candidate running for political office has a solution for the ills of the public education system. Once elected, many officials are effective in passing legislation to bring about the simplistic solutions designed by laymen to solve the complex problems of schooling in a pluralistic society in which all students are deemed equal by the Constitution. Students are not born equal in intellect or opportunity to learn. The problems inherent in the situation are made worse when the field is immersed in political scapegoating.

Renewal under these circumstances is almost impossible.

Still, the educational system is one of the most powerful institutions in existence. Schools have been described as buildings with the future inside. As imperfect as we may be for the future of humanity, we are a most powerful profession!

If the 15,000 school districts in the nation were to band together in the common cause of system renewal, and if boards, teachers' associations, administrators, and support staff were to accept the challenge of cooperation, trust, teamwork, and renewal rather than taking the adversarial positions typically seen, we could create the school learning environment idealistically described by many theorists as an educational nirvana (Glines, 1987).

There are systems in which the climate is close to the one described as open (Halpin and Croft, 1963). These are the systems that are consistently identified as exemplary, where renewal is a way of life, not the exception.

STABILITY IN MOTION

Stability in a school system promotes feelings of security. Staff working in a stable system show more confidence and are more relaxed. There is less anxiety. When a system is unstable, the staff tend to keep their heads down and go about their work in an unobtrusive manner. Stability is usually preferable to instability.

However, administrators should be on constant guard against a system which has gone beyond stability and could be described as lethargic. A system where habit and routine are the norm may be one where "group grope" is the order of the day.

The trick for the administrator is to maintain stability in the system while promoting growth. Waterman (1987) refers to it as stability in motion. In systems which can be characterized as having stability in motion, system renewal is supported.

In these systems, there is a feeling of fluidity. All things are possible. A new idea really doesn't have to wait until next year's budget is developed to be supported. If it is worthwhile, if it will improve the quality of the instructional program, the resources to support it are found. To do less is to risk stagnation.

At the other end of the continuum, there is a concerted attempt to maintain the appropriate balance between change and stability. Too much change, too fast, can destroy a system. The results can be more devastating than no change at all. In systems where stability in motion is the norm, there is a serious attempt to reduce the bureaucratic nature of the system. If the planning process can be short-circuited without taking away from the effectiveness of the proposed change, then it is done.

The system does not maintain rules for the sake of rules, paperwork for the sake of paperwork, and reports for the sake of reports. Procedures, practices, rules, and regulations are designed to facilitate the growth and improvement of the system, not to hamper it. Periodically, all rules and regulations are reviewed to be sure they are still appropriate.

ATTITUDES AND ATTENTION

The school effectiveness research is replete with the message that students respond to high expectations. If teachers set high goals for students and provide the appropriate instruction to achieve those goals, students usually respond. Most winning athletic teams are examples of this statement. If the coach's expectations of the players on a team are low, the results are clearly depicted on the scoreboard. Stories abound of skilled coaches who took a group of roughly talented kids and produced a championship team.

It applies to the school workplace and to teachers in exactly the same way. If teachers are expected to arrive on time, be well-planned, have attractive rooms, and present motivating lessons, they tend to respond accordingly. If few expectations are set by the administration, few are met.

Provide the staff with a questionnaire in which they can state what they want from the system and, almost without exception, teachers say they want more time from the administrators. Administrators wanting to promote renewal are administrators who find ways to spend individual one-on-one time with staff members. Every administrator's day should include some specified time to be spent one-to-one with staff. Most effective administrators find this to be the most profitable time of their day. Generally, one sweep through a building will reveal more information than two hours of reading reports.

An administrator of a building or a district symbolizes whatever that building stands for. If it stands for staff growth and renewal, the administrator is out and about, talking, listening, and supporting.

CAUSES AND COMMITMENT

Everyone needs a cause. The right cause can unify a faculty and be the focus for system renewal. It is important for faculty to have a cause that is uplifting, achievable, worthwhile, and fun. Something to get the creative juices flowing again. Things to think about and talk about in the teachers' room.

If the cause is one the system can buy into, then commitment to the cause follows quickly. No one cause is right for every school or every person in a school, but the administrator who supports and promotes renewal has an inclination toward identifying causes for which teachers quickly give their support.

Careful thought should be given to what the building or district cause should be for a given year. It may be called a theme. It could be a goal for the year. Whatever it is, it can become a year-long activity to promote involvement, discussion, reflection, and improvement.

Renewers are not only able to select a cause for which there will be commitment, but also seem to be able to select those which offer enough challenges to enlist commitment from the staff. The competitive instinct is aroused. Can we do it? Will we succeed? There is an element of risk that is stimulating.

This action alone can cause enough creative tension to stimulate many forms of renewal.

SUMMARY

The cornerstone of the career stages model for improvement of the teaching cadre is renewal. To obtain the maximum benefit from renewal activities, there should be a deliberate effort which is part of a strategic plan. Such a plan is a desired vision of where the school district or a school should be at some point in the future.

INQUIRY

Questions and Answers About Chapter Ten

Question #1: *Don't you see that the "rock the boat" attitude required of school administrators to install the concept of renewal is contradictory to how some school systems select administrators? What can be done about this?*

Answer: The answer requires the board to come to grips with exactly what type of administrative leadership is desired. Is the district interested in maintaining the status quo? The skills of the maintenance administrator are far different from the skills of the leader capable of renewal. The board will have to decide if it is willing to take the negative feedback that comes with opening up a system, making it fluid, and facilitating renewal. The same question will have to be answered by the central administration when it comes to hiring building-level administrators.

Question #2: *What are the obstacles you've encountered in installing renewal in a school system? How did you overcome them?*

Answer: The greatest obstacle is the lack of trust among the subgroups in the system. This is especially true of the relationship between teachers and administrators. The development of trust takes time, honest communication, and administrative behavior which genuinely supports teachers. The second greatest obstacle is the lack of human development skills among practicing administrators. The authoritative administrator is obsolete when it comes to implementing a human development model. "Do as I say, because I said it" approaches are insulting to true professional educators. The process may have to begin, not with the training of the teaching staff, but the retraining of the administrative staff. The third greatest problem is financial—finding the money to support these efforts. It takes a board willing to include a line item in the budget sufficiently large enough to fund renewal efforts. This problem is usually overcome when the board begins to see the initial results. If the funds are simply not there, it may be necessary to write grants, seeking alternate sources of funds to support the effort. Finally, it takes administrators committed to the objective, those with an attitude of "whatever it takes to accomplish the task."

Question #3: *Don't you think that many school administrators are already doing* *some of the things you've described? If so, what are the implications for the career stages concept?*

Answer: Certainly, many administrators are already doing many of the things suggested here. The beauty of this model is that they now have a framework in which to place these activities. Much of the acceptance of the Madeline Hunter model can be traced to the same reasoning. Expert/master teachers were already doing those things. The direct instruction model provided new terminology and linking the model to learning theory gave it credibility. Since administrators are already engaged in many of these activities, they have a natural knowledge base with which to link the model. This should facilitate the implementation of the model. It has been my experience that administrators easily relate to the model and can see quickly how to relate their staff development activities to it. It has also been my experience that administrators see how the model applies to themselves. They, too, can be classified as anticipatory, expert/master administrators or administrators in withdrawal. Because they can internalize the model themselves, they see its relevance.

REFERENCES

Ansoff, I. *Strategic Management.* New York:John Wiley and Sons (1979).

Black, J. and F. English. *What They Don't Tell You in Schools of Education about School Administration.* Lancaster, Pennsylvania:Technomic Publishing Company, Inc. (1986).

Cibulka, J. "Theories of Education Budgeting: Lessons from the Management of Decline," *Educational Administration Quarterly,* (1), pp. 7–40 (Winter, 1987).

English, F. and B. Steffy. "Curriculum as a Strategic Management Tool," *Educational Leadership,* pp. 276–278 (May, 1982).

Glines, D. "Looking to the 21st Century: Principals with Vision Needed to Make Schools Exciting Places of Learning," *Bulletin,* (71), pp. 92–101 (November, 1987).

Grace, L., R. Buser and D. Stuck. "What Works and What Doesn't: Characteristics of Outstanding Administrators," *Bulletin,* (71), pp. 72–76 (November ,1987).

Halpin, A. and D. Croft. *The Organizational Climate of Schools.* Chicago: University of Chicago, Midwest Administration Center (1963).

Keefe, J. "How Do You Find the Time?" In *Rethinking Reform: The Principal's Dilemma,* H. Walberg and J. Keefe (eds.). Reston, Virginia:National Association of Secondary School Principals, pp. 31–38 (1986).

Naisbitt, J. *Megatrends: Ten New Directions Transforming Our Lives.* New York:Warner Books (1982).

Waterman, R. *The Renewal Factor.* New York:Bantam Books (1987).

Index

About the Author

Betty E. Steffy is currently serving as Deputy Superintendent of Instruction in the Kentucky Department of Education, Frankfort, Kentucky. She received her B.A., M.A.T., and Ed.D. from the University of Pittsburgh.

She began her teaching career in the early seventies as a classroom teacher in the Allegheny Valley School District, Cheswick, Pennsylvania. She worked in the Division of Teacher Development at the University of Pittsburgh for three years.

Dr. Steffy began her administrative career in 1979 when she became the Director of Curriculum for the Allegheny Intermediate Unit in Pittsburgh. Later she moved to the Lynbrook Union Free School District on Long Island, New York where she was the Assistant Superintendent of Schools. She capped her administrative career by serving as Superintendent of Schools for three years of the Moorestown Township Public Schools, Moorestown, New Jersey.

She has co-authored two prior books, one being the national best seller released by the American Association of School Administrators, *Skills for Successful School Leaders*, now in a second edition.

In 1985 she was selected by the *Executive Educator* magazine as one of the one hundred national educators to watch by ten national experts on eleven criteria. She has served as a national speaker for AASA and the Association of Supervision and Curriculum Development.